SAGE TALKS

SAGE TALKS
Conversations with Gods, Deities, and Avatars

Kingsley L. Dennis

AEON

First published in 2026 by
Aeon Books

British Library Cataloguing in Publication Data

A C.I.P. for this book is available from the British Library

ISBN-13: 978-1-80152-210-6

Typeset by Medlar Publishing Solutions Pvt Ltd, India

www.aeonbooks.co.uk

In memory and celebration of a loving soul

Ibolya Katalin Kapta
(1972–2024)

The gods are indeed many …
—Basilides the Young

Imagination is the star in man
—Paracelsus

Every god is a star
—Anon

A sage in classical philosophy is someone who has attained the wisdom which a philosopher seeks. It is said that the philosopher does not have the wisdom sought, while the sage, on the other hand, does not love or seek wisdom, for it is already possessed.

According to the Greek philosopher Socrates, the two categories of persons who do not partake in philosophy are:

Gods and sages—*because they are wise.*
Senseless people—*because they think they are wise.*

CONTENTS

INTRODUCTION

WHERE HAVE ALL THE GODS GONE?

The world we see is the myth we are in

—Patrick Harpur, *The Philosopher's Secret Fire*

When we look up into the night sky and see the sparkle of stars, we are awed and enchanted. There is grace, there is wonder, and there is the excitement of the unknown. Everything comes alive with possibility. There is an enchanted world out there, and it beckons to us through a communal mystery. And we wish to respond to that call, for underlying all life is the urge for meaning. As human beings, we long for—we *need*—a sense of meaning and purpose in our lives. An enchanted universe serves to entice us with a feeling of belonging. Yet somewhere along the way we lost the sense of communion.

There was a time ("Once upon a time ...") when humanity felt a common destiny with its abode, both terrestrial and cosmic, and this encouraged a mode of direct participation. Long ago, humankind experienced its habitat as an immersive space, an inclusive matrix that involved the individual in each moment of life. Our ancestors did not stand away from life—they participated directly in its enchantment. They were a part of life and not apart from it. This merger between being and abode established a psychic wholeness in humans. Our ancestors were not estranged from the world in the way that modern humanity is. In the last few centuries especially, humankind has increasingly expunged itself out of its own mystery and thrown itself out of the realm of enchantment. Modern scientific, rational consciousness is an alienated consciousness, afraid of its participation. It views the world as an outside observer; a world of objects that move in mechanical motion. This alienated consciousness has substituted enchantment and mystery with a smear of artificiality. The cosmos of human "being and belonging" thus became tainted with the contagion of the rational (or left-brained) human mind. Yet this is not how things are. It is only the latest picture of how things *seem to us*. We have been forced into constructing our meanings about a world we have let slip away from us. In other words, we have disenchanted ourselves from a living cosmos.

The modern landscape is now more scattered with administration than adventure. The inner psychological landscape of so many people has become infected with this weary contagion. We have now been put on guard to protect our psychic spaces, and to fend off forces that, intentionally or not, serve to damage and plunge our thoughts into despair. The game playing that has become a dominant part of our lives divorces us from our real sense of self, which then quietly retreats further inward into the deep recesses of our being. Modern life is now rife with false selves parading as authentic entities. This disenchantment has become a leading lens that looks out at the world around us—and at the cosmos too. We are told that everything is just one grand accident, a colossal conglomeration of chance and chaos. And this, we are constantly told, is just how life is.

The modern history of the industrialising world has been about the removal of mystery, mind, and magic from the realm around us. Modern Western consciousness defines itself by its very removal from the world "beyond". It also unfairly labels all past thinking as not only incorrect, but primitive. That is, we tell ourselves that our understanding of the world has developed and improved in a linear fashion. Thus, all earlier thinking, concepts, and ideas were inferior and "unscientific". Humankind has erroneously defined itself on a belief of linear progress, which is mechanical and immature. Previous worldviews are seen as misguided, illegitimate, and lacking sophistication. And yet, we wonder little about how our descendants will look back upon our own current prognosis.

Whether we call our present age the modern or postmodern, the underlying current is the same. So many people seem to be spending their lives not in fear of what may happen to them, but in fear that nothing will happen to them. This malaise has, for many, been turned into an expression of anger and harm, both self-directed and towards others. It is ironic that the very institutions of learning and meaning have recently (in the US predominantly) become the very sites of violence, terror, and meaningless murder. This psychic space, where reality and unreality are in conflict, is a response to, and/or a reflection of, our dominant state of consciousness. The consciousness of each age makes its diagnosis, and often unfairly dismisses what came before. For example, we find it extremely difficult to have a grasp upon the consciousness of premodern human society. We can think with our current mental apparatus, yet we are unable to enter into a previous state of consciousness. Hence, the two modes of verification are of different worlds, literally.

The modern scientific-rational paradigm, like the religious paradigm of the seventeenth century, now finds itself unable to be maintained. This is how things unfold; one set of structures, systems, and viewpoints are eventually outmoded and, through necessity (among other factors) get replaced, or rather updated, by a new set. This new set then defines the dominant consciousness for the new era. In such moments of sociocultural transformation, when bases of knowledge are revised and our constructions of reality questioned, the need to seek the self grows stronger in the individual. In such transitional times there is urgency, opportunity, and an interior push to reconnect with a sense of meaning, both personal and cosmic. During such times of change and uncertainty, the impulse for meaning and significance becomes a more prominent and necessary urge. In other words, there is a fundamental need to understand one's self and its place in the larger scheme of things. The instability we encounter in the world around us only convinces us further of the need to find the roots that connect us with a more permanent stream of knowledge and meaning.

Once upon a time ...

Once upon a time ... when conscious, reflective thought arose within humanity, all our mental enquiries were unified into a single stream that was an inherently sacred quest. We longed to know the origins of existence. Philosophy and science were once the same endeavour, and they existed alongside a metaphysical thirst. The human spirit longed to seek beyond the rhythm of the stars and their orbits. Our ancestors watched and tracked the cycles of day and night, the great arc of star-sprinkled skies, and the heavenly revolutions. From this they calculated a measurement of time, mathematics, and reason. And with these tools they expanded the mind's reach to traverse the possibilities of life with its whys and wherefores, endlessly searching once again for the original stream of our origins. It is the spirit that seeks and calls out, wishing to know and be known, and it is society that clothes the spirit in coloured rags that change with each season's fashions. We've come to wear so many layers upon us that we hardly have any remembrance of being naked. And yet the soul of humanity, the soul of the world, has never ceased to be the essential driver that propels us further.

For thousands of years in cultures across the globe—from the ancient Egyptians to Mesoamerica—divination, myth, ritual, and direct interaction with the gods all formed part of the holistic human experience. Dealings with phenomena beyond materiality informed the psychological and spiritual development of human beings. Such mythology constituted a healthy and integral part of human consciousness. Such a premodern consciousness was also one where the ego was kept in check by the presence of powerful transcendental forces that were believed to play a permanent part in human lives. Such transcendental powers were perceived as being the real players behind human existence. And such powers were not only acting upon human beings externally but also formed a part of their interior psyche. As such, aspects of the individual—their thoughts, feelings, desires, and intentions—were not as strongly developed and manifested as they are today. In such ancient times, humankind was not considered apart from such powers, energies, or influences in the way that the modern individual believes today. This integration within the cosmological order created a natural sense of enchantment.

Yet by the first century CE, the essayist Plutarch was asking, "Why is it that the gods are no longer speaking to us?" By that time, there had been a steep decline in the prestige of the oracles and the divination that was once held so prominent in Greek culture. However, a great majority of people still believed that their lives, both internal and external, were influenced by forces beyond them, those forces which also infused their souls. For millennia the boundaries between inner and outer, and between subjective and objective, had become blurred. One did not know where to place the dividing lines, if indeed there were any. The external world of nature and the inner world of the human psyche were inextricably merged, and both were spiritualised in their own ways. And yet the process of separation was already under way. Rather than being inextricably bound together, the realms became seen as attached through forms of correspondence.

The medieval world—coming after the premodern (or antiquity), and before the modern period—contained within it a stream of consciousness that retained a link to the notion of correspondence. In this context, correspondence implied that things of the world had relations of sympathy between them. Just as women attract men, minerals meld with other minerals, and molecules attach together, so too do sympathies exist between elements of the cosmos and the earth—a Hermetic "as above, so below" set of relationships. Resemblance and sympathy were known aspects in the medieval mindset, although the Church orders worked hard to expel them on charges of heresy. Thus, many of these practices were termed "occult" and driven underground.

The modern mind wished to take a step back and to see things in isolation, and not to confuse the relation of things. Those minds that could not agree on the "consensus" relations were deemed mad or paranoiac. A famous example in literature appears in Cervantes' *Don Quixote* when his character sees the windmills as giants. In his world, things "did not compute", as we now say. Where there was no consensus programming, the social order saw this as a threat. Or rather, in the medieval world it was a threat to religious order. And thus, the understanding of correspondences eventually went into survival mode and slipped below the external membrane of medieval life. And through this, the Middle Ages grew stagnant, as there was little movement in creative vision, myth, and the innovative ideas that propelled cultures forward.

Human consciousness over the centuries has been undergoing a decoupling from the world around it; a distancing that has been referred to by the German philosopher Friedrich Schiller as "disgodding" from nature. This involves our human nonparticipation with an integral cosmos and creating a distance between human beings and everything else. In short, humanity succeeded in taking itself out of the picture by creating a new and different picture of itself. The rejection of the earlier participatory consciousness, often referred to as animism, owes a debt to the emergence of institutionalised forms of religious belief. It also owes a debt to the rationalistic side of Greek thought and philosophy that aimed to push aside instinct in favour of observation and experimentation, which eventually became the basis for a new scientific revolution many centuries later.

The Scientific Revolution of seventeenth century Western Europe established a new way of perceiving reality. An important aspect of this shift was a change from quality to quantity and from the *why* of things to the *how*. The universe, once seen as alive and having its own purposes, now became inert, a mechanical moratorium of meaningless matter. Nature became a thing to be probed and controlled, stepped back from and observed, rather than as something to merge with and participate in. Being at home in the cosmos became relegated to romantic fantasies, as purposive manipulation of the environment took its place on the human playing field. The deliberate commodity management of the world replaced the enchanted wonder of a magical life. Humanity had made a complete turnabout from participant (early humankind) to passive observers (religious revolution), to material manipulators (Scientific Revolution). The ideas of the Scientific Revolution were put fully into play during the industrial revolutions. A psychological shift also occurred that dramatically affected the individual. The closed medieval world, with its feudal structure, country folk, religious order, and close networks, provided a psychologically safe and secure environment. The advent of the rationalist era changed all this when it threw the individual mind into a brutal world of merciless mechanism, management, and meaningless industrial, urban landscapes. The individual of the new modern Europe lost their purposeful footing in the race for industrial expansion in an uncaring universe.

The ecumenical order of the medieval world was replaced by the new economic order. The logic and rationality of this was that when salvation and pardon could be bought by money, those with money had salvation. Economy became the divine goal for the new era of progress. Financial calculation became the new road to comprehending the once creative cosmos. A new completeness had been found that sat comfortably within the scientific, rational, industrial worldview. A new modern Europe was being constructed that viewed progress separate from the meaning and metaphysical significance of the individual. With the cosmos as something within concrete laws, the latest pioneers of humankind could continue unabated with their goals of conquest and competition. A new type of consciousness had seated itself at the forefront of human social development.

The late seventeenth and early eighteenth centuries did their best to discard, disprove, and remove the inner psychic landscape of the human being (their inner reality) as it did not adhere to the incoming programmes of capitalist commerce and industrial mechanisation, expansion, and management.

Despite the westernised mode of linear progress, human civilisation has largely been in a state of instability and crisis for several centuries. The modern schismatic consciousness that has been embraced as being "normal" has led us to the present state of world volatility. It is not about thinking straight, as we have been led to believe, but rather about thinking relational. The Cartesian-Newtonian paradigm, which split the world into parts and mechanised their relations, ruptured the necessary harmony between all things. Such a state of affairs is now nothing more than antiquated.

By the time we look back on this from a new phase of human civilisation historians will see the Cartesian-Newtonian paradigm as a relic. It will be viewed as a curiosity of mind that created rapid industrial expansion and scientific knowledge yet failed to bring real progress regarding fundamental knowledge of ourselves. Its spurt, which lasted several centuries, may be likened to a primitive rocket booster that propels a space shuttle into orbit only to be spent and cast off, to fry up and dissolve as it falls back down to earth. The last few centuries were a single evolutionary episode that ran its course. In anthropological terms, it was a mere blink of an eye. And in that blink, humanity brought itself to the brink of collapse. Yet at the very last step, we may just succeed in stepping back from this brink … if we can establish a new form of cosmic communion.

Cells within the collective mind of humankind are once again seeking solace in a new era of communion with an enchanted, sacred cosmos. We are not so much in a new age, but rather in a new gnosis, where so many revolutionary—or rather, evolutionary—strands of the enlightening fabric are weaving together to form a new tapestry. We have various mystical traditions mingling through mixed cultures and pushing ancient knowledge into the public domain; and the inner landscape of humanity is being increasingly traversed and mapped through exploratory and psychic tools. The great sacred mirror of the human self is reflecting back to us every known atom that ever sprang out of the creative matrix of existence. It is an epoch for momentum, acceleration, exposure, disclosure, invention, innovation, exploration, and gnostic understanding as never before on such a widespread scale. Despite the last gasps and squirming from certain malevolent forces, it is a truly miraculous age for us, here and now, to be witness to what is unfolding.

PRELUDE

LIFE IS A GIFT

... they are surely there, the divine people, for only we who have neither simplicity nor wisdom have denied them, and the simple of all times and the wise men of ancient times have seen them and even spoken to them. They live out their passionate lives not far off, as I think, and we shall be among them when we die if we but keep our natures simple and passionate.

—W. B. Yeats, *The Celtic Twilight*

They are surely there—the divine ones. I had always felt a correspondence with Yeats' proposition that such otherworldly beings exist but that, by and large, we had denied them. I'm not talking here about the notion of the omnipresent and omniscient "God"; I am speaking of all the other deities, or avatars, that have existed and continue to exist throughout the realms. This book is about my talks with such a varied degree of colourful characters.

In the haste of our modern lives, we have forgotten. We have forgotten so many things. I don't mean here about forgetting to get an item on the shopping list or other mundane daily items. I am referring to the "big" forgetting. We have forgotten to remember our connection to the greater cosmos and our participation with the vast canvas of existence.

We have forgotten to remember why we came here, and from where we came. We have forgotten that there are other intelligent, sacred intelligences within the greater realms that exist beyond the confines of our known material reality. And, most importantly of all, we have forgotten that we—each one of us—are a part of that Greater Family.

If anything, this book is about chatting with the family. That's how I wanted to envision it. It is nothing grand, opulent, or prophetic. It is not about "channelling" or any other popular categorisation. It is simply a recognition that we are, and always have been, connected to a grander reality. And it is about having a conversation. That's it really.

I think the ancient Greeks referred to it as talking with the muses. They also went to the temples to speak with the Oracles, often through a translator. It used to be that only specially trained people (priestesses, priests, initiates, etc.) were blessed with communing with the deities. Perhaps it was because only these people had the sufficient intention, focus, and receptivity to accept the "other voices" into their lives. And yet, these voices exist for all of us. We only need to have the correct *intention and receptivity* in order to allow the communion.

For many of us, especially in today's fast-paced, technologically driven, material world, there is no room for such "gods". They have been banished into the hinterlands, expelled from human belief and acceptance. It seems as if they have drifted away from us. But there is no time and space—no "distance"—in such matters. We can bring them back with a sincere thought and a genuine heart.

Our life here on this planet is but brief. It is a temporary stay. Soon enough, each one of us shall be checking out of our temporary hotel rooms. Everyone you have ever known, everything you have ever seen, will one day be gone too. This is a transitory realm. Nothing—or no one—either overstays or stays for too long. I heard it reported that an old sage once said that life is a gift; it is a gift of three days and two days are gone.

With one day left, can we still remember?

CONVERSATIONS

WITH GODS, DEITIES, AND AVATARS

The most wonderful aspect of life still seems to me that some coarse and crude intervention and even blatant violation can become the occasion for establishing a new order within us.

—Rainer Maria Rilke, *Letters on Life*

I

A chat with Hecate, Greek goddess of ghosts

In this first chat I wanted to ask about the times we are currently in, especially regarding the sense of "hauntingness" that many of us are feeling within society. Has a moment of "lostness" entered into our era? Since this is a theme of haunting, I thought it appropriate to reach out to Hecate, who is the Greek goddess of ghosts. This is how our first conversation unfolded.

Author (A): Hello. I would like to speak with Hecate. Is Hecate there? (*pause*) Hello?

Hecate (H): Hello. This is Hecate.

A: Thank you for connecting. I would like to speak with you on the theme of hauntingness. I don't know if that is a real word or not, but these days it seems like these are haunting times we are in.

H: A real word or not, it doesn't matter. I understand your concept. We often sense and feel in concepts, ideas. We don't need the words. Words are ineffective carriers. They are not accurate enough. But words are what you use. So, I need more clarification. What do you mean exactly?

A: Well, as I see it—or perhaps sense it—many people are now feeling somewhat lost. We are in a pace of change so rapid, with distractions, contradictions, misinformation, deliberate false information, and so many things happening around us that it seems reality is losing its focus.

H: Or that people are losing their focus?

A: Exactly. Don't you think so? I mean, this is more your area, where ghosts and phantasms roam the world.

H: Not exactly. The ghosts and phantasms of which you speak are no longer in human bodies. The things you mention concerning your physical reality do in fact concern humans. Humans have never, strictly speaking, been my domain. I find them more incomprehensible than ghosts. This is not a bad thing, mind you. Rather, what I am saying is that humans are more complex, unpredictable, and with unknown capacities that they constantly surprise us. What I think is happening right now is that they are in the throes of surprising themselves.

A: What do you mean? Now I have to ask you to clarify!

H: What I mean is that humans are very much at the centre of everything they do, and of their world. Things in their world may indeed be changing, yet it is the humans who decide how this affects them. Humans have more say in their reality than they realise.

A: And isn't this the issue? I mean, they are being misled about their own inherent capacity to act in their world and to create the reality and the future that is best for them.

H: Yes, and this has always been the case. The struggle is not so much with ghosts and hauntings but with their own ignorance. If anything, humans are being haunted by their own inability to see. As I said, humans are very much at the centre of everything; and it is from this centre that they must learn to see clearly.

A: Would you say then that humans are deceiving themselves?

H: Humans have always had a strong inclination for self-deception. This is not always a deliberate act, although it is fascinating to observe from our perspective. This self-deception most often comes from a lack of knowledge; or lack of information about their own state and potential in the world. They are a noble species that step by step, person to person, are moving towards a very different future.

A: And is this a positive, better future?

H: That is indeed the hope.

A: So where do we go from here?

H: We will have to wait and see. Humanity has to make its own choices. And this means it will have to struggle internally—both among its own people as well as within each person—to decide how it wishes to act and to move forward.

A: Yet there are also forces acting against humanity, are there not?

H: The forces that concern you and your kind are the ones that exist among you. You are your own disease as well as the cure. From what I see, you are struggling with and among yourselves. And there are those among you who prefer to keep the rest of you in ignorance. Be noble and seek your own truths. The path lies within you, and always has. Don't be distracted by your own ghosts.

A: Are you saying that we have everything we need and that everything is going to work out fine in the end?

H: You are simplifying here and placing into what you call neat categorisations. This is another characteristic of human behaviour. Having the tools you need is not the same as knowing you have them. And knowing you have them is not the same as knowing how to use them. Regarding the future, nothing is fixed. You live more by belief and imagination.

A: Ah yes, thanks. I spoke a little hastily there. Now what do you mean by belief and imagination?

H: Well, nothing in your realms is *already as it is*. It's difficult to translate this into words. There is *being* which always is, yet the structures for this—your lives on the planet, your civilisation, and your futures—well, these are products of what come from within you. You asked at the beginning about hauntingness as if there was a lack of meaning, or a sense of meaningless. This is a false thing—it simply is not so. Everything *is* meaning. And so, everything *already is meaningful*. There is meaning even in false things. Their falsity is itself their meaning. Even when living within ignorance we can take that ignorance as a site for meaning. You must learn to understand things from their fragments. The life you are living, this reality you dwell within, is not perfect by any means. In fact, it is flawed. And yet this imperfection is the realm from where meaning is generated. I would say that your sense of hauntingness is because you have made the visible invisible in your reality. In its place you have made non-important things the visible.

A: Meaning?

H: (*laughs*) Meaning that the meaning is within you. If there is a lack of meaning in your life it is because you have not brought this meaning forth through yourself.

A: So, it all comes from us?

H: Of course! Where else?

A: Some may say from a Creator God or a similar Divine Source, for example.

H: And what is the Created? If people choose to say that it all comes from a Creator God, then you are this Creation and so this God must work through you. And then we are back to belief and imagination.

A: Ah yes, I had almost forgotten.

H: Forgetting is another major issue of you humans, but let's not get into that here. And why say "almost forgotten" when you had forgotten? These are all the little deceptions you play with yourselves (*laughs*). Anyway, I move on. Belief and imagination work in similar ways. You choose an idea or concept and you manifest it. Belief works by becoming something you want to be true, or to exist; and imagination is something you wish to come true or make happen. They are similar mechanisms and yet they operate in different ways through your mental systems. Belief tends to be used more for blocking than for moving ahead. And imagination tends to be regarded as something not true or not existing even though its purpose is to make something exist. You have confused yourselves with these operations. This is perhaps why you are also confused with meaning. You don't know *what* gives meaning. You're looking under rocks for the sunlight.

A: Mm, yes. There's a lot to think about there.

H: Don't think on it too much or you'll destroy it! (*laughs*)

A: You seem to be fairly, well, I don't know exactly how to say it. You're jovial, or joyful for a goddess of ghosts. I expected you'd be more mournful.

H: These are your expectations and have nothing to do with me, thankfully! These are yet again your blocks. You place something in your minds and your group mental sets and then these become like concrete blocks. You walk heavy with such weight in your minds.

A: Yes, I suspect you are right. Thanks for that. And thank you for the chat, Hecate. I've enjoyed it.

H: You're welcome. That shall be all for now. Goodbye.

A: Goodbye.

Reflections

We live in a mental universe that seems to reflect our own inner movements. We have created beliefs that then create us back, either compelling us forward, or blocking and even pushing us back. Life, or that which happens between birth and death in this reality, is not a random affair of casual events. Things are connected, and events have significance even if we cannot see this or fail to see it. We are in a Game of Life, and we are all players. This "game" has many potentials for experience, including suffering and pain. And the game is temporary too. We may refer to it as the "Hidden Game" since so much of it is either hidden or non-visible to us. We play among the peaks of the icebergs while the great body lies below our visible waterline. How we choose to move through this terrain is exactly how we choose to play our game.

We console ourselves through our own deceptions. Much of how we see ourselves is a self-delusion. Many of our delusions become the world we see and in which we play. And there are many who rarely question this. Beliefs and images create the reality that we indulge in—or indulges us. As protagonists within this game, we hardly question enough.

We don't like things to be simple. If they are simple, we then imagine them to be wrong. How can such a simple thing be so right? This is so often said, and more often thought. Maybe we are just complexifying ourselves, layer upon layer. The simple, the essential, stays deep within us.

A tale

A simple truth

One day there was a mayor who decided that he could, and would, make all the inhabitants of his city observe the truth. He devised a plan that would make them all practise truthfulness.

Now to enter the mayor's city you had to cross over a bridge. And upon this bridge the mayor built some gallows. Soon after, when all was complete, the city gates were reopened and the captain of the guard was stationed with a squad of troops to examine all who entered.

An announcement was made: "Everyone will be questioned. If they tell the truth, they will be allowed to enter. If anyone lies, they will be hanged."

A simple farmer stepped forward.

"Where are you going and what is your business?"

"I am on my way to be hanged," replied the farmer.

"We don't believe you!"

"Very well, if I have told a lie, hang me!"

"But if we hang you for lying," replied the captain of the guard, "we will have made what you said be the truth!"

"That's right: now you know what truth is—YOUR truth!"

II

A chat with Momus, Greek god of satire and mockery

In this second chat I wished to continue upon the theme of society and our current lives. I decided to move away from the theme of haunting and to ask about what could be called the "strangeness" of our lives. I thought that it would perhaps be a good idea to have another perspective on our lives. For some unknown reason I suddenly had the idea of Momus in my mind; and knowing that he was the Greek god of satire and mockery I thought it might be appropriate to ask his views upon this subject. This is how the conversation went.

Author (A): Hello. I wish to have a conversation with Momus. I would like to connect with Momus. Momus?

Momus (M): Howdy there! Momus is here, loud and clear. I cannot promise anything, but we can have a chat anyway. What is it you want with me?

A: Ah, good. Thank you for agreeing to have a little chat.

M: No problem, buddy. I'm always up for a chat, and my tongue is as sharp as ever. That's what got me thrown out from keeping godly company. I guess they didn't like the hard truths! (*laughs*)

A: I guess not. And I also sense that you see clearly the strangeness of human society?

M: Aye, you could say that. Or, rather than saying strangeness, which is typically a human understatement, I'd say I see the unfairness, the oppression, the stupidity, and every other nook and cranny that runs through your games. You have the unenviable ability to amuse yourselves to death. Well, if that's how you want to play it, so be it (*whistles*).

A: Well, I'm not sure if that's exactly how we want to play it, as you say. On the whole, most of us prefer to go down the road of progress with values, ethics, and dignity.

M: (*sound of hands clapping*) Bravo, you play your part well. Please, take a bow!

A: Come on, I don't mean like that.

M: Then don't come across all pompous like.

A: I didn't think I was.

M: Then start thinking! It doesn't matter what you say; you have over six thousand living languages and they're all just a bunch of words. Words are just fragments that can't tell a story properly. How are you going to find your inheritance if you're still fumbling with words? Action, my good man—action!

A: Yes, of course, there needs to be action.

M: Arghh, don't bore me! You're just throwing words back in my face. Do I look like I'm urinating in the wind? Come on, you, get with it! I mean humans can only be taken seriously through their actions. It doesn't matter what they say or what they write—it's what they do that really counts. You have to judge a person by their actions, and not their gabble.

A: Yes, that's right.

M: So damn right, it is! (*laughs*) Most of you lot down there say one thing and then do another. It drives me mad. I've been trying to figure it out for centuries. I even got to the point where my brain began to hurt. Imagine that! And now I think I have the answer, although it's not a very profound one.

A: And what is that?

M: It is simply that you're not aware you're doing it; for most of the time anyway. You actually believe that what you say is the same as what you do. You completely lack awareness in this matter. It's like you have a blind spot, or some blockage within you that simply refuses to see it. What you lack as a species is awareness. Hey there—get aware. Wake up!

A: And how does one wake up?

M: (*laughs and sound of hands clapping*) How "does one" … does one? What goes with you man, did you suddenly swallow a delusional pill that made you think you were a king? What's with this royal "one"? You see what I'm saying? You're so attached to your words that you dress up in them like royalty.

A: (*laughing*) Okay then, how do we wake up? Come on, give it to me straight.

M: What do you expect—that I'm going to give it to you bendy? You have to wake up; you've got to crack some eggs and dance with the chickens. Nobody's going to do it for you. Stop being lazy and start being smart. Great things are expected from you lot. Don't keep us hanging around. There's a large company of us waiting on you guys.

A: What do you mean by waiting on us?

M: What, you think you're alone there? Well, I guess you do. First you run with the gods and then you dump them. You act as if you can do anything. You think you're living in a vacuum where nothing else matters. I sometimes roll in laughter watching you all strut about with your heads high. You want to know why there's strangeness in your societies? Well, that's *you*! You're the only strange things on this planet. Everything else fits in perfectly. Everything else has a place. Now you guys, you're lumbering about without a clue. That's why I'm so busy. It's your manifestations that gives me things to mock. What I satirise is yourselves. That's part of why I'm here. You needed someone, or something, to show these things back to you.

A: So it all comes back to us then. We are the laughing stock?

M: If you want to put it that way. But don't get all pitying about this. It's all a good thing—in the end, anyway. You are sometimes the laughing stock, other times the way-showers and the warriors. You can be all these things. But it's the pompous stuff that really sets you back.

A: Our self-importance you mean?

M: Righty so. And all of the arrogance that comes with it. Why do you have to act this way? In every age you wear the dress that matches your attitudes. Watch and observe this. See how you dress. And in these clothes you also wear your personalities. It's like you're going to a big ball, pompously strutting around trying to impress others. Why can't you just chill. Know that everything is here for you as you are, in your essence. Everything in the world supports you. All of Nature and all the beings in your world—they want you to find yourselves too. They want to help. But you're all blind.

A: That's what I mean. I want to know how we can wake up from this blindness. I don't want it any more than you.

M: Then stop taking yourselves so seriously. Step back and step down. Like yourself and like others. And always do your best without hurting others. Life is not a race. It's a walking path. Walk on it, but not like a peacock! Walk like a human being. Grateful and humble. Otherwise you're gonna receive some serious mocking from me.

A: Okay, got it. Thanks. So, any more advice?

M: Sure. Get moving and stop waffling. And that's on the house!

A: (*laughs*) Thanks, Momus.

M: No worries. Anyway, got to run. Nice chatting with you, although you weren't the smartest cookie. Ciao …

A: Cheers for that.

Reflections

It's somewhat humbling to speak with such other voices. Even though I can't say for sure their origin, they at least have an interesting angle of observation. I find what they say helpful in looking at ourselves. I'm reminded that one of the impossibilities in our lives is to look upon our own face directly. We can see it through a mirror or through photographs and videos; yet never directly with our own eyes. It is the major

"I" that we wear throughout our lives. I always think of my face as being "me". It is what defines me to the other people I meet. When people don't know who you are they learn to recognise you from your face. We are now being profiled by "facial recognition" software that will come to define us. We become deeply serious about the way we look. Or, as Momus put it, through the way we dress.

It seems that we also define ourselves by the dress, or clothes we wear. Maybe from another perspective it does indeed look as if we are strutting about, like peacocks. I think the bottom line here is that we need to be able to laugh at ourselves. We are both the laughing stock as well as divine stock.

Do we take ourselves too seriously? Maybe the answer to this is out there in the world. Look at what's going on. Is there arrogance? Ignorance? Self-importance?

It says in the Zohar that "Man, whilst in this world, considers not and reflects not what he is standing on, and each day as it passes, he regards as though it has vanished into nothingness." The mockery of all this is that we don't see, or perceive, what we have or what is right before our eyes. Mockery can be a mirror to shine upon ourselves; like a mockingbird mimicking our call back to us. We should learn to listen more.

We should also be aware of our capacity to deceive ourselves with our own explanations for truth.

A tale

The explanation

Three explorers—a priest, a businessman, and a mystic—were passing through a dangerous jungle. As the journey continued the jungle became increasingly dangerous. As each day passed the animals appeared larger, more hostile, and eventually began to follow the three explorers.

Eventually the three explorers had to take refuge by climbing up a tree for fear they would be attacked. After convening a council to discuss the situation they decided that one of them would have to go and seek help. After all, they could only stay up in the tree so many days before they succumbed to hunger, thirst, and fatigue. And none of the explorers wished to fall into the mouth of a ravenous beast below. But they could not decide which one of them should go.

"Not me," said the priest. "I am a servant of God and I need to stay behind to comfort the remaining person."

"Well, certainly not me," said the businessman, "because I am paying for the trip!"

The mystic said nothing, but then suddenly pushed the priest off from the tree. The priest fell to the ground. Immediately a ferocious pack of wolves surrounded the priest but instead of attacking him they defended him against the rest of the hungry animals. After fighting off the rest, they placed the priest on the back of their largest wolf and carefully escorted him to safety.

"It's a miracle!" cried the businessman. "After all your cruelty, divine intervention decided to save that good man. And this has also restored my faith in a holy life."

"Hold on, not so fast," said the mystic. "There is in fact another explanation for what you see."

"What other explanation can there possibly be?" shouted the businessman angrily.

"Simply this—that it takes one to know one," replied the mystic, "and that the smallest always recognise their leader and honour him ..."

III

A chat with Janus, Roman god of beginnings, transitions, passages, and endings

This third chat further explores some of the questions regarding human society, especially in their relationship to a larger framework. Society, and our place in it, has its own internal systems; yet surely, there are bigger cycles going on. I decided to ask questions on this topic. So, I called upon Janus who is the Roman god of beginnings, transitions, passages, and endings.

Author (A): Hello, I am wishing to communicate with Janus. Can I connect with Janus? (*pause*)

Janus (J): Greetings. This is Janus.

A: Greetings to you, Janus. Your arrival is very welcome, and fitting regarding what I wanted to talk about.

J: Yes. My timing is always appropriate. That is why I am the god and patron of beginnings, transitions, and endings. And what kind of a god of beginnings and endings would I be if I had no sense of correct timing? You would not wish for a beginning to be delayed or an ending to come too soon, would you?

A: Quite so. And it is fitting because it was beginnings and endings that I wished to talk about.

J: Naturally, that is why I am here and you are here. You humans may think everything in your life is a random coincidence, but from our perspective it is not. I suggest you try the bigger perspective some time. It would greatly benefit you.

A: Thank you. Yes, I have been striving for a sense of the bigger picture most of my life. It's not easy when you're a human. We tend to live our whole lives with what's just in front of our eyes. My grandparents never lived anywhere else except the town where they were born. And we all grow up with the ideas planted in us by our parents and community. Human lives are often sheltered in this way. There is seldom any sense of the bigger picture. Now the world is different. People being born into the world today are more naturally hardwired for a bigger-picture perspective.

J: That is correct. Many of you humans had a larger perspective in your history. That is, in your earlier years. Yet this larger perspective was often aligned with either a mythological or a religious-mystical view. You always relied upon a delivery method, something to bring these larger views to you. That is also one of the reasons why we came to you in the guise of gods. You were unable to receive information unless it corresponded to specific parameters of thinking. And for a long time in your human history these parameters were what you would call "quasi-religious". You were unable to see alone, through your own senses. Your intelligence was attached to certain cultural forms. That is why everything, even today, must be delivered to you in an *appropriate* way.

A: And what would happen if this information arrived to us in ways that were not "appropriate"?

J: As has always been the case. The information is either rejected or the carrier—the way of transmission—is attacked. That is why those of us whom you call "gods" also have to appear to you in ways that you can assimilate within certain of your psychological patterns. And this is how we are communicating right now. You have this mental framework of a god called Janus, who represents a range of functions. And this is who I am to you.

A: And who are you to others, or to yourself?

J: This is neither relevant nor useful to you right now. So, back to your initial question. Tell me what it is about beginnings and endings that you wished to know of.

A: Well, I understand that phases in human history have their cycles—their beginnings and endings—and that at certain times, in particular epochs, we pass through a transition period that is especially momentous. Isn't that so?

J: Yes, that is so; according to how your reality operates through matter. The cycles that operate within your realm have, more or less, always been in this way. These patterns have always been there for your historians to see. They are like programmes that are self-regulating and can be left to continue on their own. These unfoldings, or transitions, also mark the passages of time for you upon the planet. That is, these beginnings and endings are time-markers for your reality. They provide the sense of linear sequence. Or what you call progress and development. Other domains have their own passages and transitions too; although beginnings and endings are something that is specific to your dimensional realm.

A: And why is that?

J: It is because experience within your reality is perceived as being linear. This is largely an earth-bound perspective. And at the two-, and even three-dimensional level this perspective is largely correct. However, it is inaccurate and a very limited understanding. Yet it works for where you are at now. Without going into detail, I can say that outside your constrictive reality there is no sense of beginning and end—everything is connected and conceptual, not linear. By perceiving sequence, you are able to see things in specific positions. Because you have yet to develop a consciousness of correspondence where everything is related, you are given to perceive things in positions. To put it another way, in your modern terminology, you see the islands but not the underlying water that connects them. In your terms, you understand a movement from one place to another. In this way, one door closes and another opens.

A: Yes, I think I get that. And that is also what I wanted to ask. My sense is that right now, using this terminology, we are closing one door upon our history and are opening another. I mean, we are opening a doorway into a new epoch and so we are in that transition from stepping out of one doorway and entering into another. Is that so?

J: Yes, it is. Of course, this is only true from the perspective that pertains to your reality. And you have made these crossings many times before in your long history. Some of them were made before what you call your "history" even began. But now I speak only of your current phase in human civilisation. It is an important transition that you are currently in.

A: Yes, I feel this. And I'm sure I am not alone here. There are many people who feel similar about our present epoch. Can you tell me why this is so?

J: I can explain a little; only so much as to not affect the agency of free will among your species.

A: Okay, thanks. Please go ahead.

J: There is a convergence of many areas of change, and they have all come together at the same time. Some of them concern your social systems and historic forces, as is normal. Yet there are other changes occurring within the human being itself that will provide an extra ingredient. I can tell you that you are also changing from within, from the very fibre of your bodies. All this will affect your human consciousness. And thirdly, there is change occurring within your planet as she adjusts to prepare for her new position in space and energy. All these factors together are resulting in what your historians will look back on and call a "historic period" of change. This moment in your history will never be forgotten, just as you have not forgotten the Scientific Revolution or the end of your medieval period. You have been in a modern dark age, despite your industrial growth and technologies. Within your human experience, regarding the awareness of your soul aspect, you have still been as if in the dark ages. Now all that is set to change. Have you understood?

A: Yes. Well, I understand what you say; although I'm not sure if I fully understand the workings of it.

J: That is correct, and to be expected. There will be few humans who will understand the true nature of the transition upon this planet. There are reasons for this, but they do not concern you.

A: Yes, okay. Could you say something more about us being in the modern dark ages?

J: Yes. You often confuse consciousness with matter. Your paradigms of growth, development and progress are all matter-based. That is, they are materialistic paradigms. They do not correlate to true awareness, knowledge, or understanding. How you manipulate matter, which are your objects, is not a question of true progress. The end of the medieval Dark Ages brought you out of mythology and superstition and into matter, so to speak. Then your industrial ages gave you the means and tools to develop your relationship with things of matter. Yet you have ignored that which truly matters—and this is consciousness. Matter comes from consciousness and not the other way around. You continue to obsess yourselves with secondary phenomena. This is a sign that you are still, as a species, in the dark ages. You have yet to awaken to the true power and presence of consciousness. Until you do so you will remain within the dark, regardless of the trickery of your machines.

A: And so, this transition that you speak of is about moving us out of the dark and into an awareness of consciousness?

J: Yes, that is so. The transition that stands before you, so to speak, is a monumental one in your history as a species. It is about a recognition—an understanding—of the fundamental underlying energies of your realm. And this is a question of consciousness. This is primary. All other elements, no matter how sophisticated they are, belong to the secondary.

A: And this future towards a recognition of the fundamental reality of consciousness awaits us?

J: Yes, it does. Although I cannot give you any frames of reference in terms of time. This is flexible, and changes constantly. But rest assured that you are moving through portals, and the future that awaits you is beyond your present perceptions. I can tell you, however, that it will be beyond your imaginings. There is so much that awaits you—from one door and through another.

A: Yes, thank you. This corresponds with my own intuition. Yet right now we are experiencing turbulent times.

J: Changing tides always create turbulence in their wake. This is the pattern of all material things, as well as energetic states—both here and beyond your realm.

A: And I suppose that we shall get through this?

J: I suppose too. Although, there is much that is still in your hands, as is always the case. You, or rather your species, are responsible for stepping through the doors. Beginnings and endings exist, yet *how* you step between them is largely your own doing.

A: Yes, that is true. And would you say that as part of the bigger picture what we are experiencing now is the turbulence of crossing this current transition?

J: As part of the bigger picture, yes. It is but a brief moment within the overall movement of development upon your planet. For your human experience, however, it shall be a lifetime, or more.

A: Yes, I suspected it would be. I might not live it out, yet this is beyond just one person.

J: You and your generation will live a great deal out and will witness some great changes. Stick around, there is more to come. As some of you humans often like to say—enjoy the ride!

A: Yeah, thanks for that. I certainly will, through the rough and the smooth.

J: Indeed, it shall be both of those. Yet where you are heading is beyond words. Head up, keep looking forward, and sacred speed to you. The rest is up to you—to *all* of you. You are greater than you know. Do not downplay your ability. Deep faith and courage—and look both ways! (*low laugh*).

A: Thank you, Janus. I will. I mean, we all will—keep moving ahead, with courage. Thank you for those final words.

J: Always remember yourself. Now I say goodbye.

A: Goodbye, Janus.

Reflections

We are somewhat both blessed and cursed by the nature of time. It rules and regulates our lives as well as being a necessary marker. Time affects each one of us differently. It is right to say that "time is relative". Two lovers will pass the night more quickly than a person with toothache. For me personally, I am always checking the time. I would feel lost without a watch on my wrist. There are some people who prefer not to wear watches. There are others who prefer to check the time on their smartphone, almost constantly at the same time as checking for messages. Time is used both to measure the passing of the heavens as it is to monitor and regulate our working hours. When do we "clock-on" and "clock-off"?

Time is shifting now. The working hours are more fluid. Our own time for distinguishing between the separations of our daily lives—work, home, and leisure—are becoming blurred. Each year seems to pass quicker than the last. Or are we only growing old? Do our senses measure time differently as we age?

It is true that doors open and doors close. We are told never to miss an opportunity for they do not return. An opportunity is like a word spoken in haste—they cannot be brought back.

Human calendars are not the same as earthly or cosmic calendars. The earth has its own movement and rhythms, as do the starry heavens above us. Over time we can see trends and movements across the earth as well as in our human cycles. Ages and epochs come and go, and we name them according to their features. We have our bronze and iron ages; our agricultural and industrial; and now our technological revolutions. Some of these are doors, or portals, to a radically new "time" upon the earth. Others seem more like continuations. See how we measure everything by this thing we call "time"?

Time is only relative to us. It consists of our human measurements. It gives us justification as well as a position in the grand scheme of things. It also makes us hurry and defines our meanings and our sense of wasting the little "time" we have in this fleeting life.

A tale

Wasted time

A wise queen gazed out over her kingdom. She was content knowing that she had dedicated her life in service to her land and its people. The kingdom had grown into stability and harmony. Yet the queen was concerned that perhaps some of the people had become complacent. She decided that she would announce a competition. She would give a bag of gold to the person who could demonstrate the most unusual thing.

Word soon spread over the kingdom and in the coming weeks people came from near and far to the queen's court in order to show off their "unusual thing". There were people who walked on hands or danced in the strangest of ways. One person played like a flute through their fluttering fingers. Another sang like a nightingale while another warbled like a mockingbird. The queen enjoyed the show, yet nothing came close to being the most unusual.

Finally, one day an old man entered the court and claimed that he could thread a needle from 30 metres. The queen raised her eyebrows in disbelief. If the old man could surely achieve this, then it would indeed be the most unusual thing. Accordingly, the old man was allowed entry into one of the towers of the courtyard. Below a high window 30 metres up the old man positioned himself carefully. Down within the courtyard at the base of the tower stood a lady of the queen's court with a silver needle in her fingers. After a long time of waiting the old man eventually released his thread. Slowly it fell to the ground and, to everyone's astonishment, it fell directly through the eye of the needle. The court was amazed and cheered the old man.

As soon as the old man had come down the tower the queen presented him with his reward—a bag full of gold. "Tell me," said the queen. "How did you achieve this most unusual feat?"

"Highness," replied the old man somewhat proudly, "I have been practising this all my life. I have climbed high trees for over fifty years and each day I practised."

"And your family? Your job?" enquired the queen.

The old man shook his head. "I was too busy practising threading the needle to be concerned with such things. Yet finally I did it," said the man with a smile. "And now I am rich because of it."

The queen immediately grabbed the bag of gold away from the old man. "You were rewarded the bag of gold for your unusual feat. Now I am punishing you for having wasted your life."

And the queen had the old man sent away never to be seen again.

IV

A chat with Eris, Greek goddess of strife and discord

In this fourth conversation I wished to discuss further the idea of transitions in terms of turbulence. It is apparent that right now many people are feeling a great deal of uncertainty, social agitation, and unease. Something is stirring the social melting pot. So, who better to call upon than Eris, the Greek goddess of strife and discord.

Author (A): Hello. I would like to start a conversation with the Greek goddess Eris. Hello … Eris?

Eris (E): Whoa, is that you there?

A: Yes, I think so.

E: You sound hesitant.

A: I am speaking with Eris, the goddess of strife and discord, am I not? Should I be hesitant?

E: Yes, you are. And you should be hesitant—very hesitant! (*laughs*). No, you'll be fine. I'm not here to cause any more wars.

A: Ah yes, the famous Troy affair and the golden apple of discord. Well, let's not get started on that.

E: Yes. Let's not even go there (*giggles*). So, what's on your mind then?

A: I've been thinking recently about all the strife and discord that seems to be entering the world in recent years. I know these things have always been around, but it just seems like there is more discord than normal. I hope you've got nothing to do with all this?

E: Not likely! Besides, you don't need me around to help you; you're doing just fine creating your own discord. I'm happy to sit back and watch it unfold.

A: Lucky you. Yet down here things seem kind of weird. You know, out of kilter. There is a sense of imbalance and disharmony, and it's affecting people differently.

E: And how is it affecting you?

A: Well, I seem to be okay, thanks. As always, I'm trying to see things in perspective, and not to get pulled into the mess. A lot of it appears to be manufactured to me.

E: Well, it is and it isn't. But you're right about trying to maintain perspective. Strife has always been around; it is part of the tug and pull of life. In fact, ironic as it sounds, strife is often needed before harmony and coherence.

A: How's that?

E: It's quite simple. The cosmos as you know it is forever being pulled towards greater coherence. Yet discord is a prime driver in this. This is natural discord which exists for order to come about—if you get my meaning?

A: Sure, I can understand that order comes out of chaos, as they say. So some strife is necessary. But that's natural discord, isn't it?

E: Yes, it is natural in that it is part of the underlying laws of your reality and the cosmos reflects this. Of course, we must be clear here. When I talk about "natural" I am referring to those laws governing *your* realm. These are not "natural" to us. Yet by knowing how the natural laws operate in your realm is useful. It helps to see things on a grander level, and to know that discord is not necessarily a bad thing. There are unsettlings, so to speak, so that things can come together later on. Think of it as planting. First you need to prepare the soil. Perhaps you need to plough it, to turn over the earth, before you can plant for the new season. There are energies, and cycles, that have this function. Some of your kind are aware of this, although mostly this goes unsuspected.

A: And what about the manufactured stuff?

E: Ah, well—that *is* your problem! (*laughs*). It's all about power. You've got some folks down there with you who don't want to let go of their power structures. They're the old guard and they're not happy about the incoming changes.

A: So, that means then that some good change is on its way?

E: Oh yeah, you've got some fun times ahead. But believe me kid, there's a few bumps coming your way first. But it's all energy, and you're receiving some decent sized energy blasts in your path.

A: And that's a good thing?

E: It will be eventually. However, again I have to say that it's difficult for us to use these terms of "good" and "bad". How can you know what's good for you if you can't see further than your own nose, as you people like to say?

A: That's a good point. Again, I guess it's a relative thing.

E: Relative, yes, as all things are. And what might be useful for one person may damage the other. Discord and strife are occurrences that need to pass, in the larger scheme of things. And they will pass. Sometimes interventions are required for a little chaos to erupt in order to spur things into motion. That is where I often come into the picture.

A: The golden apple episode?

E: (*laughs*) Oh yeah, such as the golden apple. It's all part of the game, no matter how spontaneous it looks from smaller eyes. Anyway, for you my dears, there's going to be a few disruptive waves that will rock your boats as well as propelling you forward, which is their function. There's so much new stuff coming down the line. The problem is that there are a lot of mean people down there who don't want to accept the coming flows. As you say, they don't want to get off the line. But they're going to get pushed off. Whoosh!

A: In the meantime, the rest of us have to keep our balance.

E: You got it. Stay sane and don't get distracted by all the discord that's being pushed your way.

A: That's exactly what I say. Don't get taken in by all the fear mongering.

E: Yes, there's going to be a lot of that. They're going to be throwing it all around the place—fear here, tyranny there. But these are the actions of desperate people. They're on the way out; and with strategies like that they need to be! War has been an active feature on your planet. Violence can also be functional or non-essential. There are times when warfare erupts on your planet due to influences that are beyond you. These are cosmic forces that you are largely unaware of. Let's just call them the friction of the planets. A bad energy washes over your planet and aggravates circumstances. What you refer to as warfare is both an aggravation as well as a cure for the aggravation. Again, hard to really explain this. Then there are the petty wars which many of your power-hungry personalities have started. And that is just childish.

A: Nothing like a classy golden apple to get a war started.

E: (*laughs*) Yes, that was classy of me, I do admit. Yet don't believe the history—or the hype! It was actually a pre-planned and required act that I accepted to fulfil. These are just some of the things that we folks have to do as service. I just got landed with the golden apple. But it could have been a lot worse. I mean, there have been worse! (*laughs*) The problem here, as you rightly alluded to, is when to recognise the discord as resulting from "natural" movements in your cosmos and when it is the result of human-made manufactured events.

A: And is it easy to distinguish the difference?

E: Not when you are an automaton, or a programmed person within the mass system. This is why distraction techniques are used. You guys are being bombarded right now with one distraction event after the next. In fact, they are no longer episodic but occurring simultaneously. This constant discordant stimulus is creating continual attention events so your focus is on the smaller physical playground. So few of you people are even cognisant of cosmic processes in play. You've forgotten your so-called gods, so how are you even going to remember anything outside your bubble. Sorry to say this, but humankind exists in a kind of perceptual containment.

A: And being within this perceptual containment makes it difficult for people to understand or comprehend that larger forces are operating within this realm that may, from time to time, be the cause of energetic imbalance, resulting in strife.

E: Exactly so. And what is not recognised or understood is largely ignored. And what remains? The manufactured, physical disruptions remain. This makes you think that only a human "physical solution" is the answer. But wrong again! The answer is going to come from a place you least expect. And you can quote me on that one! But anyway kid, just hang on and don't get duped by the fear. Remember, you're better than that. Good luck with it all, and don't forget to smile once in a while. I'm off to make trouble over yonder! (*laughs*)

A: Thanks Eris!

Reflections

Sometimes we don't know what is good for us. We have automatic reactions to what we think we know is "good" or "bad". Neither are we aware of when strife and chaos are a consequence of the larger influences out of our control, or when they are the result of malicious human manipulations. Also, that such disruptions may even be beneficial to us is a new way of thinking. We tend to believe that all disruptions or unpleasant occurrences are bad in themselves. And yet, if such things are beyond us, should we worry? This is a question that is difficult to answer.

There may also be "interventions" that cause strife. I'm sure our varied histories are full of them. Were they all bad? All necessary? Again, there is no one answer. We are given rationalisations daily for the acts of human behaviour, and these excuses are often a betrayal against our better natures. Discord, warfare, chaos—these are all events that just seem so unreasonable. I'm sure that every balanced human being inherently wishes for peace, harmony, and cohesion. To some degree, we have become desensitised as a species: both to human atrocity as well as to the truth.

Maybe we need to get our own house in order first before we trespass upon others'. Even when there is discord around us, we can still work upon maintaining a stability within. Outer disruptions should not necessarily have free passage into our inner world, our private lives. It is hard to keep a balance when things seem crazy around us. But if we have no control over these external events, then where can we have a degree of control? Within us. We are our own gatekeepers. We choose the visitors who gain entry into our private domain. At all times we can retain a watchfulness.

We may judge that which we see, or what we are given to see, without fully knowing or appreciating what is really taking place. We should perhaps gain a modicum of awareness before leaping into the fray.

A tale

The man who swallowed a snake

An intelligent man was riding out on his horse one day through the countryside when he spotted the figure of someone sleeping. As he rode closer, he saw what appeared to be a drunken person sleeping and snoring loudly under a tree. As he watched he also saw that a snake had crawled down from the branches of the tree and entered into the mouth of the sleeping man.

Immediately the rider rode up, jumped off his horse and took his riding whip against the sleeping fellow. The man awoke with a howl of pain. He was confused and couldn't understand why someone would do such a thing.

"Get up and run, you fool!" shouted the rider.

The drowsy man struggled to his feet and began to stagger. The rider continued to whip the man to make him run faster. He followed the man, whipping him all the time, until they came to a nearby tree where many rotten apples had fallen to the floor. The rider demanded that the drunken man eat as many rotten apples as he could. He whipped him several times into obedience. The man ate out of fear, not knowing why someone would want to do such a thing to him. He pleaded to the rider, yet to no avail.

"Cruel man, let a poor man be. I have done nothing to you," he pleaded.

The rider did not listen and only whipped him harder. "Now run, faster!" he shouted.

The man continued to run around the field as he was chased and whipped by the rider until eventually, through exhaustion and all the rotten apples in his stomach, he fell down upon his knees and vomited. All of a sudden, a snake came out of him and slipped hurriedly away into the underbrush.

Then the man realised what had happened.

"If I had told you there was a snake inside you", said the rider, "you would have either thought I was lying and ignored me or become immobilised by shock. Both these actions could have killed you. There was no alternative but to do what I did, unbeknown to you."

The man knew then that the rider had perceived a greater truth unavailable to him; and he was thankful for it.

V

A chat with Sia, Egyptian god of perception

In this fifth chat, or conversation, I decided to ask questions regarding the nature of reality. Of course, this is a huge subject and not one that could be covered in one short chat. However, I wished to touch upon the subject and to see what would come of it. For this topic, I called upon Sia, the Egyptian god of perception.

Author (A): I would like to begin a conversation with Sia. (*pause*) May I speak with Sia?

Sia (S): Hey.

A: Hello Sia. Thanks for showing up. I appreciate it.

S: No worries. We're always around anyway, in one form or another. What is it you wish to talk about—anything particular on your mind?

A: Yes. I was thinking about the current reality of our lives right now. And I was thinking that the reality of life is quite a ride at this moment.

S: What do you mean?

A: Well, it just seems as if we've entered upon some kind of reality rollercoaster in recent years. And it's not clear if anyone is in control of the program.

S: Nice analogy; but aren't you overreacting?

A: That's just it, everything seems to be in overreaction mode right now. Is this how things are meant to be?

S: Mm, yeah. I see what you mean. Of course, it's very much a matter of perception too.

A: I had a feeling you might say that.

S: Then you were right. But I was going to say it all the same. I say it because it's true. Perception is everything. When you can see the truth clearly then the choices become obvious.

A: And is it possible to see the truth, as you say?

S: Possible, but not easy; nor is it something that humankind is actively seeking. Truths are one of the first casualties in your reality. I believe you have a saying; something like the first casualty of war is truth? Well, that's quite apt.

A: Yes, we do. And, ironically, that is a truth. We can also say nowadays that the first casualty of news is truth. Yet why do you say it's apt?

S: I say that because in some ways you are involved in a war right now—a war, or struggle, for which type of reality you will collectively share as a species. Your reality has always been based upon how you see it, naturally. I'm not saying anything new by telling you that you exist within a perception-based reality. The question is how you choose to perceive, and this can be a matter of self-training or of external influences. This is the battle that has always been waged. Historically speaking, this was easier as mythologies were readily accepted by the masses. In your times now, it appears that there is a lot more confusion over which stories are more believed and accepted. Or perhaps I shouldn't call them stories, as this word has too light a meaning for you. Maybe we should stick with belief systems and social narratives. Perceptions are being manipulated in your times to a very high degree. It is confusing many of you.

A: Tell me about it! It feels more and more as if we are in a form of hyperreality where the distinction between what is real and what is false is blurred. Is that not so?

S: I'm inclined to agree, for the moment. No form of reality at your level is ever fixed. We may refer to them as sub-realities for now. Since you are shifting through ages, from one stage of your civilisation to another, there is a great amount of flux and disturbance. There is also a great amount of energy coming in and playing a degree of havoc with life on your planet at the moment.

A: A great amount of energy? That sounds ominous, as well as familiar.

S: (*gentle laugh*) Well, it depends on your perception and perspective, of course. I don't really know how you would define "ominous". In your human form you tend to see all things as either one or the other. Nuances are not your strong point. Anyway, perhaps I should talk about this energy a little?

A: Yes, please do.

S: Okay. Such energy is necessary for where things are going. In what may appear paradoxical to you, from your perspective, this energy is both disruptive and stabilising.

A: Yes, I've heard something similar to this. But could you clarify more?

S: Yes, I will clarify. Imagine you pull the plug out of your bath in order to release the bathwater. There is a build-up of energy around your plughole as all the water attempts to get released. This build-up creates what seems like a vortex around the hole, no?

A: Yes, I know what you mean.

S: Well, this vortex is a stabilising form that serves to hold the pressure of the water, the energy, while it finds release and moves on to another form, or another use. Similarly, there is a great amount of energy upon your planet right now that is being utilised to assist the transformation between ages. It is both disruptive as well as being similar to a vortex and holding the energy. This formation of energy across your planet has the effect of seeming to accelerate events, such as time. This acceleration you have already alluded to as what you call "hyperreality".

A: Ah, I think I understand now. And so, this hyperreality phase will pass once the old energy has been released—out of the bath, so to speak—and a new energy has entered.

S: Correct. From your perspective this form of hyperreality is an existing and real phenomenon. Yet from my perception it is a brief moment within a larger span of time, which is necessary for the forward momentum of life and development upon your planet. Perception provides a position of distinction between seeing something as a chaotic, rushing energy, or as a dynamic but stable concentration of energy. Your reality structures are trying to accommodate these energetic fluxes.

A: Thank you, Sia, that's a helpful analogy. And do you think our reality structures will also shift?

S: Of course. Reality structures is perhaps not the best term to use here. Again, I find myself limited by a constrictive vocabulary. By structures I mean arrangements or patterns. Such a reality as you experience is more of an arrangement of patterns. These are energetic arrangements that correspond to different scales of perception. What you are able to perceive right now from your planetary perspective is quite dense. Your planet's vibration, and hence your reality, operates upon a lower plane. This will change as events pass. New forms and arrangements will come into being in accordance with different energetic correspondences. Am I making sense?

A: Yes, please go on.

S: Only to say that all forms of reality are in movement and are all-inclusive.

A: All-inclusive?

S: Yes. You participate *within* them. You are within the reality domain, or "reality bubble", as it moves and shifts, so to say.

A: And can we ever see out of this "reality bubble"?

S: Well, yes. This has been the objective of many of your wisdom paths for centuries. There are many traditions that teach and train for this. But that is another story. You also have images and renditions of this in your creative arts.

A: We do?

S: (*laughs*) Yes, you do. But *you* will have to look for them. That's your homework, let us say.

A: Yes, I know. You cannot give us everything on a plate.

S: Certainly not. Where would the learning be? Where would the fun be?

A: Indeed. So instead of going down the rabbit hole, to quote a popular phrase, we are going down the vortex of a plughole?

S: Mm. I'm not sure I totally resonate with that phrase. But I think I receive the general meaning inherent within it. You do use odd phraseology at times. It is awkward, but also somewhat amusing.

A: I'm sure it is.

S: Well, I wished to say that you are moving through what you may refer to as an energised vortex. And this will affect the nature of your sensory perceptions, although more so in the long term. As parameters of time and space are affected within your reality domain, so will your bodily structures develop sensory and perceptual organs to adapt to these changes in space-time parameters. Think of it all as a journey of discovery, and nothing is static.

A: I think it was an ancient Greek philosopher who said that *All is flux.*

S: Maybe. Although many systems of Greek learning came through from the Egyptian schools. But that is another story, as you say. Well, that's it for now.

A: Thank you, Sia.

S: No problem. And don't forget to stay the course. Goodbye.

A: Bye.

Reflections

Sometimes I feel as if I know nothing. Not in any sense of false humility but rather, to the contrary, in that everything seems so overwhelming. There is so much that lies beyond our range of the physical senses. So much exists out there beyond our "reality bubble". I sometimes wonder if we are not in some kind of mental prison. Or rather, confined within a kind of consciousness quarantine. Maybe I am overreacting, as Sia said.

When I look up at the sky, watch the clouds drift overhead, I often wonder if there is something else beyond our skies. Not just space, as we've been shown ... but something *else* beyond. What if space is just an illusion—a veil? What if all of the visible universe is just a part of our reality bubble which is self-contained? Perhaps the idea that the universe is almost infinite, always expanding outwards, is just part of the illusion. And everything within this reality has been set up to validate this illusion. It begins to feel as if we are living in some reality TV "Truman Show" type of existence. Maybe we are.

As a young boy I used to look at the night sky and the stars through a telescope, like many young kids did. Yet I used to wonder if what I was seeing out there in the dark skies was actually real—objectively real—or was just there according to my eyes. After all, were not telescopes invented to correspond to the human eye? So maybe what we can see is not related to the objective existence of a thing but rather in accordance with the human eye (our sense perceptions) to perceive it. Rather than seeing, and knowing, that which truly exists we are only seeing that which we *can* see. And beyond this lies so much more, as yet unfathomable to us.

A tale

Two worlds apart

Santiago the shepherd and his wife Lidia were accustomed to travelling from place to place with their herd of goats. Santiago and his wife were used to a life on the fringe, in both meanings of the word. They lived on the outskirts of a modern life, as they preferred to live a nomadic existence roaming the pastures of the Iberian Peninsula. Theirs was a life of soil, sky, sun, and rain. They had no television for they were not interested in the televised life of silly folk with their paranoia or their false psychotic problems for TV psychiatrists. Neither did they have smartphones for they considered it unnecessary to know the fluctuations of the stock exchange when they knew their own local market prices.

The shepherd and his wife also lived on the outskirts of the many towns and cities they passed on their regular grazing routes. They bought their small supplies of food from local markets on the outskirts too and cooked over a small fire where they would pitch their tent. The water they took from nearby brooks as they passed, or from known springs. The water was not always the cleanest, due to groundwater pollution, but it served them well.

Santiago and his wife Lidia were content with their pastoral way of life. They had everything they needed. It was a surprise then when one day while grazing their goats they came across a new spring which they had never discovered before. Upon drinking from this new source of water, it seemed to them to be the sweetest water they had ever tasted. To you and me, however, the water was sure to taste brackish and unrefined.

"This", said Santiago, "must certainly be like the water of paradise, so fresh and sweet is its taste." His wife Lidia agreed with him. "We must share this with someone who will appreciate it."

Santiago filled a goatskin full of the water and decided to head off to see the mayor of the largest city of the province. Taking with him his own few supplies Santiago travelled for a day and a half until he came to the gates of the imposing city hall. As was the weekly custom, Santiago arrived in time for when citizens were granted a public audience with the mayor.

Upon being motioned forward, Santiago proudly walked up to the large table and announced the discovery of what he called the "Water of Paradise" and his intention to offer it as a gift to the mayor in recognition of her fine public duties. "I am a poor and simple shepherd", said Santiago, "who lives with his wife on the outskirts roaming the pastures. I know of herding yet not much of other things. Modern life is a strange world for me. However, I do know good water when I taste it, and this is truly the Water of Paradise. And realising that it is fitting for those, like you, of high social rank I bring it here as an offering from my simple shepherd's heart."

The mayor took the goatskin and, with diplomacy and politeness, asked one of her aides to pour out a glass. She then told Santiago to wait to one side for her reply, as she had a line of citizens also waiting to speak with her. Later, when the crowds were gone, the mayor tasted the brackish water that was unpleasant upon her tongue. Yet as a person of experience, who knew the ways of the local people well, she understood immediately the situation. "What to us is nothing, to this shepherd is everything," she told her aides. "Therefore, take him quickly away from here before he discovers the Water of Paradise in our drinking taps and in our bathrooms. Take him to the outskirts of the city and provide him with ample food for his kindness. Further, inform him that I bestow upon both him and his wife the title of "Custodians of the Outskirts" that they may forever feel privileged in their chosen life—for the modern city is no place for the world they have chosen."

VI

A chat with Chronos, Greek god of time

For this next chat I wanted to touch upon a theme which had come up several times in the previous conversations—the notion of time. Since I had alluded to the nature of time in terms of our perceptions of reality, I wished to ask more directly upon this subject. Who better, I thought, than to approach Chronos himself, the Greek god of time.

Author (A): Hello Chronos. Are you there? I am wishing to communicate with Chronos.

Chronos (C): Greetings. I am here.

A: Thank you. First of all, I would like to say that I know there is some confusion over your identity, as you often seem to get mixed up with Kronos, the Titan father of Zeus. Yet you are an actual god of time, right?

C: (*sighs*). Ah, there are some things which time does not seem able to correct, and that confusion is one of them. It really is best if we don't go there right now. For your purposes, I am a god of time—at least in terms of time and perspective that your reality is familiar with. If I say any more on this, it will only confuse you further.

A: Okay, thank you Chronos. Apologies if I have caused any confusion over this.

C: No worries—no time lost (*low chuckle*).

A: In that case, you're the very person—sorry, god—that I need to speak with. I'd really like to get a handle on this time issue we seem to be experiencing here on earth.

C: Would you care to elaborate?

A: Sure. It seems that the human experience of time is speeding up, accelerating, and this is not just my own sensation. Peoples from all over the place are saying similar things. It just seems as if a day is no longer sufficient to do all the things we once used to do. And yet our devices that measure time record no objective difference. Is there something actually happening here, or is this just a collective delusion?

C: Collective delusions are something that humankind is very good at. However, in this case there is indeed more to it. It is interesting that you mention time as both a measurement and as a sensation, an experience. And it is both. There is no physical property of time in terms of your devices, such as the watches you put on your arms. Your days are cut into segments through your devices. What humans sense or perceive as "objective time" comes from celestial movements. These you have measured over aeons through your calendars.

A: And so, we have both artificial time as we have created and a more objective time?

C: Yes, if you wish to place them into two simple categories. On your planet throughout history, you have created measurements of time that you adopted. You chose calendars to suit your needs, to measure your social ages and your cultural cycles. Some of these were aligned with grander cosmic cycles by those people who had knowledge. Yet many of your measurements and calendars were either developed or continued by people who had no knowledge themselves. Therefore, these time devices, if you wish to call them that, became "out of time".

A: And we also changed our calendars to suit various religious movements.

C: That is so. In this context, time became a structure to regulate your social development.

A: And we still have that today in terms of social management. I mean, in how our work routines are calculated, and when we "clock on" and "clock off" for work. Time is a monitoring tool in this context.

C: That is so. This is lower-level use of your sense of linear movement. As I said, there are movements that happen within your cosmic sphere that can be aligned with to better understand what you would refer to as "time flow".

A: The flow of time?

C: Yes. This flow has presence only in your reality. It can be used as an indication, a marker. Everything, as you know, is in a state of flux.

A: And our calendars also may in fact be in a state of change?

C: Not only the calendars themselves but the phenomena which they seek to measure. Your planet does not exist in a vacuum, despite what many of your kind like to think. It has a place, and role, in a much grander scheme. And this grander cosmological scheme involves movements and changes on such a huge scale that it is beyond your understanding. However, there are effects, or rather phenomena, from these cosmological changes. These effects can be measured by those calendars that are correctly aligned with geophysical processes. The geophysical state of your planet is similarly aligned, or rather corresponds, to cosmic phenomena. But the important point is in the experience. Energetic variations that enter your interstellar and then solar neighbourhood affect certain astronomical constants.

A: So, wait a minute. You are saying that larger changes or movements in the cosmos affect the planet earth?

C: Precisely. This has always been the case. As you people like to say—this is not rocket science.

A: And that these changes may bring with them energetic affects?

C: Yes, both in energetic shifts as well as alterations in astronomical constants. Together these phenomena influence the spin of your planet and thus its energetic environment which nurtures you. You thus have geophysical impacts as well as those that affect your human nervous system. These you generally refer to as physiological and emotional impacts, or disturbances. These impacts do much more than just affect your durations, your time frequencies. They are responsible for behavioural features across your planet. Yet this is another subject. Let us stay within time, for now. Generally, you have so far been unable to measure these changes because you have yet to produce the appropriate instrumentation.

A: Yet we are feeling these changes, aren't we?

C: Indeed, you are. You could say that you are going to war over them. You are experiencing, or sensing, specific cosmological impacts that are, and always have been, influencing life and development upon your planet. These are natural occurrences. You are sensing a different quality to that which you know of as time. Yet your instruments have not picked up on this in any consistent manner. (*chuckles*)

A: Wow.

C: The more sophisticated your technologies become, the more they will find these energetic behaviours. You are already investigating what your science calls the quantum field. As you probe further … well, I should say, as your consciousness and understanding develops you will discover patterns in this time field. I call it "time field" although this is a very vague term and not altogether correct. I use it in conjunction with your vocabulary and image sense. Forgive the inaccuracies. These are not good for a god of time! (*low laugh*)

A: No, sure, it's fine—I understand. So, tell me, will these energetic impacts create a disturbance in our reality.

C: They already are and have been for some time. You often experience them through other means.

A: Such as?

C: Such as geophysical disturbances like earthquakes, eruptions, and various environmental manifestations. In your social environments through warfare, revolutions, and other cultural upheavals.

A: Oh dear.

C: Don't worry too much about this. Your species is actually hardwired to be adaptable to these changes. My suggestion to you now is that you remain grounded and stable. The last thing you need to be doing in these times is, as I believe you say, going off the rails.

A: Yes, that's right! It sure does seem like now is the perfect time to be grounded and in control of our emotions. I didn't think the subject of time would have all these associations. I started out asking about time and our calendars and we've ended up talking about earthquakes, war, and revolutions. And these are all related to time?

C: (*laughs*) Well, there is no real clear-cut thing called time, if the truth be told.

A: But you're the god of time, are you not?

C: I am. But that is the denomination you people gave to me. Again, it is a simplification in order to represent more complex issues. It might be easier to say that I—and all of us here—represent certain phenomena rather than singular features. Yet humans have always tended to personify such things. Time is a good example. It is not one thing. It is rather a phenomenon that binds and corresponds. It is integrative. Time is not one thing. As your scientists say, it is a relative thing.

A: Yes, but could you give an example?

C: Yes. You notice that your human bodies grow and then decay with the passing of this thing called time.

A: Sure. It's one of our greatest burdens.

C: Mm, well. Your body grows old, as you say, and yet you do not sense a similar passage in your inner self. This inner "you" is not affected by this passage of time. Yet the world around changes alongside the "you" but in so many different ways. Your "time" affects how you perceive and interact with the world around you. Yet this is different for everybody. You notice that things in your house start to change, or decay. Or some things even grow healthier, such as the trees in your garden. Everything has its processes, and yet you relate to them according to your sense of time. And this is completely relative. It is, to put it bluntly, how you choose to live with it.

A: So, what you are saying then is that no one can experience my time for me. It is only for me. We are all children of time.

C: Exactly!

A: Thanks, Chronos, that's been a great help. I've enjoyed our conversation.

C: You're welcome. As I always say—any time!

Reflections

We are obsessed by time. We are shaped and governed by it. We feel rushed and so tell ourselves to "take your time". Most things in our lives are framed by the notion of the measurement of time. It's true that as we grow older time seems to pass quicker. I never thought this true until I started getting older myself. Now the years pass one after the other so quickly it's becoming difficult to tell them apart. Yet internal time is different.

I still feel young inside as if I am a man in my twenties. My body, of course, tells me otherwise. I cannot know how the larger cycles of time work—cosmic cycles or planetary cycles. That is out of my range of perception. I can only feel the play of time against myself. And most of the time, I'm concerned of losing what amount of time there is left. Perhaps this helps us to live more in the present as it is the moment that is closest to us. Yet when I feel most in the present, the sense of time disappears. It is the *Now*.

Maybe true existence is within the everlasting present. There isn't anything else but the *Isness of Now*.

I'm certain that our perspectives on time are what befuddles our lives sometimes. We hoard or save; we hold out or hold back. We refrain from saying those most needed words. We delay sharing our hearts. And then the moment passes and is gone. Time then becomes a regret.

I would now say that in order to know how to live properly, we first need to learn how to understand time—and to embrace it.

A tale

The angel of death

A miser had accumulated, by effort, trade, and lending, five million pounds. He had lands and buildings, and all kinds of wealth. He then decided that he would spend a year in enjoyment, living comfortably, and then decide as to what his future should be.

But, almost as soon as he had stopped amassing money the Angel of Death appeared before him, to take his life away.

The miser tried, by every argument which he could muster, to dissuade the angel, who seemed, however, adamant. Then the man said: "Grant me but three more days and I will give you one-third of my possessions."

The angel refused, and pulled again at the miser's life, tugging to take it away. Then the man said:

"If you only allow me two more days on earth, I will give you two hundred thousand pounds from my vault." But the angel would not listen to him. And the angel even refused to give the man a solitary extra day for all his five million pounds. The miser then said:

"Please, then, give me just one hour more of life!" Again, the angel refused. Desperate, the man begged for five minutes more, yet the Angel of Death refused.

"Just one minute more, please! Just give me time enough to write one little thing down."

This time the angel allowed him this single concession, and the man wrote, with his own blood:

Man, make use of your life. I could not even buy one minute for five million pounds. Make sure that you realise the value of your time.

VII

A chat with Aranyani, Hindu goddess of the forests

For this seventh chat I wanted to move away from talk on reality and cycles and to shift towards something closer to home—our relationship with Nature. Without doubt, humanity has, by and large, distanced and alienated itself from a deep relationship with the natural world. This is the bane of modern life it seems. I wished to talk to somebody on this. I called upon Aranyani, the Hindu goddess of the forests.

Author (A): Hello Aranyani. Can I speak with you—are you there?

Aranyani (Ai): (*short pause*) Hello … hello!

A: Hello Aranyani. How are you today?

Ai: Today? Why today? I don't have days like you do.

A: Ah yes, sorry. I was thinking in my own terms of time. It's a frequent trap!

Ai: That's okay, we understand. Traps are there to break out of. I am good, thank you. I am well.

A: That is good to hear. I am glad to know you are well amid all this disconnection going on right now.

Ai: Disconnection? I am gently strolling through my forests. There is no disconnection. (*another short pause*) All is well here.

A: Sorry, I should have been more specific. I meant disconnection between us humans and the natural world. It seems that we've done a terrible job of respecting Nature and our environment.

Ai: Mm, yes, that is so. I am not fond of strolling too near to your civilisations. But why do you call it a job? You see, already you show a wrong way to look at things. Your way of words shows how your mind thinks. Looking after the natural world, as you put it, is not a "job". It is a recognition of respect, or mutual interdependence, and of compassion and love.

A: Sorry again. I know that I use my words too loosely. It is the way we use phrases here.

Ai: Yes, I know how humanity is. For one thing, you don't listen at all very well. You consider yourselves as a separate species. My dear, nothing is separate. When you gaze out you see space between bodies, and you label this as separation. You think and behave like children, and Nature is your forgiving mother.

A: I know, we've got a lot of things back-to-front. Would you care to explain more on this relationship?

Ai: (*a soft sigh*) Maybe a little. Everything is in communication and always has been. You don't necessarily need a mouth or words or letters to communicate. It all communicates energetically, and you humans are also attuned to this. Every part was supposed to work together. You are strange in that you forgot how to listen properly. And now you build devices outside yourselves to wrap around the earth—but you don't need them. And there will be a time when you shall know this, and learn to communicate correctly, as you were always meant to—and not with your machine things. All of nature is alive, don't you know that?

A: Yes, some of us do; but not enough, unfortunately.

Ai: You knew better before, a long time ago.

A: Yes, I have a feeling we did. Yet we now need to learn how to think in a different way.

Ai: Well … (*long pause*)

A: Hello, are you there Aranyani?

Ai: Oh yes, sorry, I was dancing. I have a tune in my head. It's been given to me from the trees.

A: Wonderful! I was saying that we need to learn how to think in a different way.

Ai: That's not really how it is. Learning, thinking, and all these things—it's all head stuff. You live too much in your heads. You always think you need to grab and grasp onto something in order to know it better. I would say you have to open up more, and to remember everything that was placed inside you. You are coming to a different place now.

A: Yes, thank you. And what do you mean by "coming to a different place"?

Ai: I mean you are not in your little tribal units anymore. You are now all over the earth. You grew and connected—as you should—and now you are coming to a time when you can really be of help to the earth.

A: You mean as a global species?

Ai: (*laughs*) You and your fancy words. Yes, you are connecting more strongly with the body of Gaia now. Soon you will find your minds being changed for you. That should be fun!

A: Ah, and what do you mean by that?

Ai: (*hums to herself*) I don't feel I should reveal too much just now. Not too many of you have realised that your minds are attuned to Gaia, your planet consciousness. Consciousness is not only those thoughts in your head, silly! (*laughs*) This is the true language, the natural language, and it is everywhere. This language flows through the trees, the plants, the animals, and through all of Gaia. There is a language that connects, and the humans are disconnected from this. Yes, that is the true disconnection. You talk about a disconnect from Nature, but really it is disconnection from your shared language. You speak in tongues but only babble silly words.

A: Yes, true—we do babble a lot.

Ai: Babble, babble, yes you do! Like that story you tell yourselves. You call it the Tower of Babel, right?

A: Yes, that's true. And it's a perfect analogy. We tried to build a tower to our Creator and we ended up being divided in languages through our ignorance.

Ai: Yes, that's it right there. You were disconnected through your ignorance.

A: Mm … yes.

Ai: Don't worry, dear. You still have it all inside you. Your connection to Origin and the universal language is still there. And you are not disconnected from us either. You are always with us, and you always have been.

A: Okay, sure. And thanks. Yet despite being with you always, are we still not making the balance of Nature worse?

Ai: Oh, dear ones—it's always about you, isn't it? Let me tell you that Nature is far more capable of taking care of herself than you are. Things change, yes. And you are making a mess and not clearing up your mess, like children. This is indeed true. Yet so many more things come to pass that are not in your hands—*that* is Nature. She is so far beyond your comprehension of her. You think of these separate things within Nature, like the trees and the forests, and the rivers. But you cannot yet see them as being all together as a wondrous Being. She is a Being far beyond your little minds. And she cares for you. Little children, wake up!

A: Yes, yes.

Ai: Be more joyful and love the things you have, and which surround you. The disconnection you speak of is less from Nature and more from yourselves (*starts to sing*)

A: That is so true—thank you.

Ai: I have to go now … byeee (*voice fades into distance*)

A: Yes, thank you Aranyani. Goodbye!

Reflections

It is always about us. That was a good point made there. Life is very much about us. We are anthropocentric. That is, human beings believe they are the most important thing in the universe. What we call "our reality" revolves around our human values and experiences. Everything around us, all that we see, is based on us and our values. This is anthropocentrism and it's always been how we've seen the world. It is also myopic—that is, short-sighted.

In our worldview, Nature doesn't have a being or a belonging. That's how the dominant story goes. No wonder we're losing out every time to her. We're tripping over our own feet. It's true: we are still children.

There is a shared language that all living beings speak. But we're not speaking it. Every form is an expression of language. Every living thing is also in communication. Language and communication dictates form and anatomy. It has been discovered that if a plant is transplanted to a different ecosystem, it will transform its anatomy so as to adapt to a new context of communication. Language—the message, the word—adapts the anatomy of the carrier. We are all carriers of a specific message, and our language is more than the word; it is also the energy, the spirit, the communion of the cosmos.

Yet we have forgotten how to listen. Instead, we tune our ears to the rubbish that is filtering through our societies. We have become deaf to the primordial language. We have replaced it with babble, trivia, and blah blah blah. It means we don't participate. And it's a shame. We are a shared family, but we've ostracised ourselves.

For now.

I sense the whole cosmos resonates with forgiveness. Be joyful and love the things we have. That's a nice way to end a conversation. The final point is telling, though. We are more disconnected from ourselves.

We can do harm to other beings around us, yet in truth we are doing it to ourselves. We are not separate. Everything comes back to the doer. Everything comes back to source—to Origin.

We're on a path to find ourselves, and every other living being is participating in this game to help us. It is the hidden game. Well, it is hidden from *us* anyway.

For now.

A tale

Use of the tongue

There was a king who had the most beautiful daughter and everyone in his kingdom loved his daughter, both for her kindness and her beauty. Soon the time came for the daughter to be given in marriage. The king was at a loss of how to decide on a suitable match for his beloved daughter. He called his vizier to him who was not only a trusted aide but also a wise dervish.

"Sire," said the vizier dervish. "I shall set three tasks to complete. Whoever completes these tasks with truth shall be the one whom your daughter shall marry." The king agreed this was a good idea. The vizier whispered into the king's ear.

"But these are only two tasks!" replied the king.

"Wait, Sire, for I shall disclose the third after the first two have been completed. We need patience in this." The king agreed.

Soon the king announced that he was going to set tasks to the suitors who had gathered in hope of persuading the king for his daughter's hand in marriage.

"Whoever can succeed in all of them," said the king, "will be worthy to marry my daughter." Then he set the first task. "I want each suitor to go out and bring me the sweetest thing in the kingdom."

The following day all the suitors returned. The king received each of them in turn, with his daughter standing silently behind him. As each suitor, dressed in fine clothes, approached the king they said a greeting to the princess. Yet she remained with head bowed, not looking up.

Some brought the sweetest flowers from across the kingdom. Others brought bowls of the sweetest honey that anyone had tasted. Each person brought an item of some sweet thing in order to please the king. Finally, at the end of the queue was a poor young man whom nobody had paid any attention to, for not only was he dressed meekly but also he carried nothing with him. When it came to his turn he stood before the king and bowed. Yet he did not greet the princess. After a moment of silence, the princess raised her eyes and met those of the young man. Still, he said nothing.

"Well, what is your sweet offering?" asked the king, somewhat impatiently. The young man bent his head forward and stuck out his tongue. "Ah, what

mockery is this?! How dare you insult the king—I shall have you flogged. Guards!"

At this point the vizier stepped in from the side and bowed to the king. "Sire, may we not first ask this young man what he meant by his actions? I feel there is more here than meets the eye." The king agreed and demanded an explanation from the young man.

"I bring you a tongue," he replied. "For a tongue can truly be the sweetest thing in the world. If sweet words are delivered by the tongue then they can make a sick person well, an unhappy person happy. They can bring joy and meaning into life where before there was none. The sweetness of the tongue can carry compassion from the human heart."

The king was taken aback by what he heard. He had to agree that in this sweetness there was truth.

Next the king announced the second task. "I want each suitor to go out and bring me the bitterest thing in the kingdom."

The following day all the suitors returned and once again the king received each of them in turn. As each suitor brought their item, whether a bitter fruit, a bitter herb or plant, they each greeted the princess. Again, she did not look up. Finally, at the end of the queue came the poor young man. And again, he carried nothing in his hands. When he approached the king he did not greet the princess but remained in silence. After a pause the princess raised her eyes and met those of the young man. Still, he said nothing.

"Well, what is your bitterest offering?" asked the king, somewhat impatiently. The young man bent his head forward and stuck out his tongue. "Ah, again, what joke is this you make of me. You have insulted me yet another time—I shall have you hanged. Guards!"

At this point the vizier once again stepped in from the side and bowed to the king. "Sire, may we not first ask this young man what he meant by his actions? I feel there is more here than meets the eye." The king agreed and demanded an explanation from the young man.

"I bring you a tongue," he replied. "For a tongue can truly be the bitterest thing in the world. If it says bitter words then it can make the happiest person sad. It also has the power the break a heart. Is this not the bitterest thing?"

The king thought about his daughter's heart breaking and then had to agree that such a thing would be the bitterest indeed. Yet again, the poor young man had completed his task over those of the other suitors.

Now the king turned to the vizier and asked for the third task. The vizier asked to king to accompany him into the royal kitchens.

"Sire, I shall now make you a cup of coffee." The vizier proceeded to place some embers from the wood-burning stove onto the bowl that heated the water above for the coffee. Then he leant in close to the water as it bubbled. "Mmm, yes," said the vizier.

"What is it?" asked the king impatiently.

"The water is saying something, listen to it. What is the water saying?"

The king came forward to listen, but all he could hear was the sound of bubbles. A blank look stretched across his face. The vizier came close and whispered in his ear for a few moments.

A broad smile leaped across the king's face. "Aha, that poor boy will never know this answer. He will never know what boiling water is saying. He isn't educated enough to find an answer to complete this final task!" Immediately the king returned to court and announced to all gathered that the final task was to tell him what the water is saying as it bubbles over a heat.

All the suitors looked aghast, including the poor young man who went home despondent. Who could know the truth of this question?

Now close to the kitchen was one of the king's servants who was cleaning. She was a kind lady and well-liked by the princess. So she ran to tell the princess what she had overheard in the kitchen. Later than evening, as the king lay resting in his chambers his daughter the princess came and offered to make him a coffee. He agreed and soon the daughter returned with the coffee as she had suggested. Upon handing it to her father she remarked casually—"As I was making the coffee I listened to the sound of the water as it boiled. I got to thinking, I wonder what this water is saying. If only I could know what it means?"

"Ah, my daughter, I can tell you what it's saying," he said hastily. "The water is saying that I was a drop in a cloud. Then when there was condensation the cloud opened and I fell to earth as a drop of rain. As this drop of rain I landed on fertile soil where a seed had been planted. I watered this seed which then grew into a tree. Later a woodcutter came to chop the tree down and make it into

firewood which he sold at market. This wood was then placed in the stove from where the embers were taken and placed in the bowl which boiled the water. And so, I am saying that 'What is burning me is from me'." The king sat back and smiled proudly.

The daughter nodded but showed no great reaction. She said goodnight and left. When she returned to her room she wrote down everything her father the king had spoken in haste. The next morning, she instructed her trusted servant to find the house of the poor young man and to deliver her letter to him. Because just as the young man was in love with the princess, so was she taken by the silent gaze of this young man.

The next day the suitors lined up and one after the other they all told their fantastical tales of invention about what the water could be saying. "The water says 'I am the king's servant'," said one suitor. "The water says 'I boil to bring life to the kingdom'," said another. The king dismissed all of these fawning replies. Finally, the young man approached the king and this time he did not stick out his tongue. Instead, leaning forward, he spoke softly and told the story just as the princess had related it. Finally, he added—"And the water is saying that 'What is burning me is from me'."

The king's face turned bright red. He was dumbstruck. Finally, he said "Ah, now I see that what is burning me is from me!"

And that is how a poor young man came to be married to a princess and finally became king himself. And his word was respected, for everyone in the kingdom took the king's word on trust.

VIII

A chat with Ptah, Egyptian god of craftsmen

For this chat I decided to approach the subject of creativity. I had on my mind the notion of technology and how creativity is now shifting into the realm of humans becoming a different form of "creator". For this theme, I called upon Ptah, the Egyptian god of craftsmen.

Author (A): Hello Ptah? Hello, are you there?

Ptah (P): I am (*deep voice*)

A: Ah, thank you. So, you are the god of craftsmen then?

P: I am indeed—of all the crafts: metalworking, sculpture, carpentry, construction. All craftsmen create, and I am the patron of creation.

A: Wonderful.

P: Why is that so? Are you a craftsman—one who creates?

A: Well, in a way. I try to create through the craft of words. I work a different way with my hands; but yes, I still create.

P: There are many ways to create. Some are through hard working of the hands, and I have dealt much with these persons. I understand also there is creation through projection of thoughts and through transcribing. I have guided your craftsmen for many ages. You have capacity for invention, and for curiosity.

A: Yes, when we transcribe the ideas that come into our minds, it is like a craft. The word is itself a craft. We are only the carriers.

P: Ah yes, that is so.

A: And it's the curiosity which is our strength, and perhaps our weakness.

P: Your meaning?

A: There is a strong push now to move from craftsmanship to a different form of creation. Our scientists are exploring bioengineering, creating new biological and hybrid organisms. And our computer scientists are attempting to create machine intelligence.

P: The cosmos is filled with intelligence. Why should you feel that you have the sole right to it?

A: I don't. I'm fully aware we are not the only species to manifest intelligence. What I'm wondering is whether we should be the ones to create another form of intelligence.

P: You yourselves were created. Do you not see a pattern?

A: Well, I wasn't talking about a god here.

P: Neither was I. There is creation and intelligence at all levels. Your whole planet is not only filled with intelligence but is intelligence itself. Intelligence is universal. It is everything that is. There is nothing that does not exhibit a form of intelligence. Why do you always hearken back to your idea of gods?

A: Well, that's a good point because it brings up the issue of humans playing at being gods.

P: (*low deep chuckle*) Yes, you do like to play. But leave the gods out of this one. Creation, and the ability to create, is one of the wondrous aspects of your cosmos. You do not need to think of yourselves as gods to create. Do children building sandcastles think of themselves as gods?

A: Maybe not—but we are hardly talking about sandcastles here.

P: Yet you are building all the same. Let me tell you something—*you* do not create conscious intelligence. It already exists. You only create vessels to receive it. Let go of your arrogance and pride. You are not able to get within an inch of creating consciousness. Without the gift of the cosmos, you yourselves are but machines, reacting to stimuli. You were given a gift. And you are not the ones to decide if and when that gift should be bestowed. Create—experiment!—and in doing so you will have the opportunity to understand your own humanity.

A: Good advice.

P: I'm not giving advice. I am not a counsellor. I speak what I know to be my truths—take them or leave them, as humans have always done.

A: I should speak with you more often.

P: Don't think so highly of yourself—I'm doing you a favour.

A: Right, got it.

P: Anything else? Your dimension is not conducive to me. Being here too long brings back arduous memories … (*low murmur*)

A: Oh, okay. I won't keep you much longer then, just a final question about technology. Are humans doing the right thing in their continued development of "smart" technologies?

P: That question does not mean much to me. It tells me more about your own thinking, which is not yet of a high enough level to grasp the issues of which we can speak.

A: Mm … okay. But could we give it a try?

P: Briefly. You speak of both technology and smart. These are concepts which are relative to your own time-space matrix. Technology is a term you overly misuse. In a sense, everything is a technology—including the human race. You seem to think technology is just something metallic or artificial. I tell you now that all of life in your cosmos is a form of technology. Smart—this is such an obscure term it has no sense. You think people are smart because their brains can retain information. You wrongly define the sense you wish to convey here. I would suggest you consider this notion in terms of being closer to or further from the Truth. Smart is a social ranking system you have—it bears no relation to your conscious self. Finally, are you doing the right thing? Haven't you ever heard of free will? That's why we mostly leave your planet alone. Not the best of ideas, in my humble opinion. Well, that is all.

A: Well, thank you, Ptah. You have given me much to consider.

P: Perhaps you may now consider on how to ask more appropriate questions.

A: Yes, I will certainly work on that. Thank you.

P: I go.

A: Goodbye.

Reflections

Again, we seem to think that everything comes from us. It is *we* who create, rather than understanding that creation is a flow. It appears to be a human trait that automatically, without much thinking, we generalise that most things start from us. Perhaps we should see it in terms of a relational engagement. We can participate in the flow, like joining the currents of the river. Or, likewise, we can act as the blockage of that flow. If this happens too often then we become as jetsam—the debris deliberately thrown into the waters.

Creation and creativity are a flow, like inspiration. And we must be ready for it. I like the now-famous quote from the painter Picasso who said: "*Inspiration exists, but it has to find you working.*" We can't sit around waiting for miracles or magic to just suddenly happen. We've got to be running for that train.

Also, humans generally think that they are smart. Yet smartness may just be our ranking system after all. And we place these values onto those things we create. That's the issue here—we are the ones placing "our values" onto the other, whether it be person or machine. Yet if we are only half-filled with partial or relative truths, then what are we truly imparting?

Let us hope we are not creating tools with prejudices!

A tale

A meeting of tools

It is told that there was once a carpentry workshop where all the tools held a meeting to settle their differences. At the head of this strange assembly was the hammer acting as president, but soon the other tools declared that he had to resign because he made too much noise with his blows. Hammer admitted the charge, but he refused to resign from the presidency because it would mess up the organisation, and if the screw took over, as he was wanting to do, this would only screw things up and make the meeting chaotic and without order. The screw and all kinds of nuts argued against this at the same time objecting against the sandpaper taking the presidency as this would create excessive friction with his usual rough abrasive treatment. Others agreed with this also saying that the tape measure should be thrown out the meeting as he always measured others according to a fixed pattern, as if he were the only one perfect.

Finally, the carpenter arrived at the workshop, and placing his apron upon himself set about his work. He used the hammer, sandpaper, tape measure, nuts and screws. Finally, the initial block of rough wood turned into a beautiful and useful piece of furniture. When the work was finished the carpenter silently left the room, and once again the tools' meeting was resumed. That's when the saw began to speak; he said:

"Friends, it has been shown to us that we each have our flaws, but the carpenter works with our qualities—that's what makes us valuable. Let us not think more on the negatives we see in each other; rather let us see our skills that we each contribute, and which the carpenter appreciates and uses to the best."

The assembly then realised that the hammer was strong and gave force to the screw; sandpaper was able to polish and smooth things over; and that the tape measure was accurate and precise. Together, they were a team capable of producing high quality furniture. This made them proud of their strengths and capable of working together. And from then on everyone became the best they could and worked in harmony to create the most beautiful and functional furniture one could ever hope to find.

IX

A chat with Hermes, Greek god of travel, thievery, and trickery

I started here by thinking about the idea of our boundaries. About how we artificially create such things as our separations and distinctions; and how we then spend the rest of our time investing in those things we've just established. I thought maybe it's a type of trickery we play upon ourselves. For this reason, I decided to call upon Hermes, the Greek god of such things as trickery.

Author (A): I wish to begin a conversation with Hermes. Hello Hermes, are you there? (*indistinct noise*) Hello?

Hermes (H): Ahoy there. Hermes is indeed here!

A: Great, I wasn't sure if you'd turn up. I heard you are hard to get hold of.

H: (*laughs*) Ah, you've been listening to my detractors! I'm always around. You know, I don't think there is ever a still moment.

A: Well, you are the messenger for the gods; and you are the god for travellers and for boundaries. I guess that means you are always on the move.

H: So true, so true. I'm always zipping here or there. There are really no boundaries where I go. And if there are, well, I just cross over all of them. I must confess, I don't get these boundaries everyone talks about. All worlds and realms intermingle, whether under or over or through. (*chuckles*)

A: Actually, that's something I wanted to talk with you about. Our world here is full of boundaries, and many of them are invented. I refer to it as a simulation. Someone, or let's say a nation, comes over and draws a boundary on a map. Then you have a new space. But it's just a story that then becomes history.

H: Yeah, sure, tell me about it. I see you humans doing this all the time. We give you an open, clean slate and then you go drawing all over it, inventing your new rules for each game. You literally take out a pen and then it's a line here, a line there. You keep changing the lines and then changing the rules. We all thought you were a schizophrenic lot until we came to realise it was an infantile learning process. You expel a lot of energy in these territorial games.

A: Do you think it is all a simulation?

H: What does that really mean? Everything is a simulation in one way or another. A simulation is just something that is a copy or reflection from the Real. So, sure it is. But that doesn't take its validity away. I deal with what you call simulations all the time, and it's real enough for many intelligences. It is what you have made from your slice of reality. You then make a subset of simulations within the bigger simulation. It's a kind of trickery really, but it can also take you further away from where you need to be.

A: And I suppose trickery is your game, with you being Hermes the Trickster, right?

H: (*laughs*) Sure thing! But all the trickery I do is for a purpose. And much of it has been to help you guys out. Didn't you know that? I've done lots of trickery but generally for your well-being. But now many of you are enjoying what you call sleight-of-hand for your own selfish ends. This is not real trickery, sorry to say. It is manipulation, and there are many of you who love this game.

A: And how do you see this type of trickery—this manipulation?

H: Like I said, it's infantile from where we see things. It is more thievery than trickery. Everyone seems to be telling lies to each other, and you are building up a reality that steals the truth away. Every layer of lies that you put out takes you further from your connection to the Real. You are putting veils over yourselves and smiling while you do it. It's not clever, whatever you may think.

A: No, not clever at all. Manipulations and lies are never clever. But there are those people who think it is. I think they feel it gives them power.

H: Power, perhaps. Yet power is only a game. And like I said, this game takes you further from yourselves. I think maybe you're getting lost in your own game.

A: That's interesting. Do you think we are also creating borders for ourselves?

H: Without a doubt! In the early days you had Heaven and Hell. Now you have everything in-between too. Borders are made real by your imaginings. Your world exists first in your head; then you manifest and express it into something real outside of your heads. Your borders are your power lines. There are no borders from where I'm watching. I see a bunch of children playing in their school playground. You are sitting in your sandpits building fake castles and walls that are soon to fall. If you build with the wrong intention, then such things will never last. And what's more, they will collapse on top of you. You'll be a bunch of children submerged by your sand games!

A: What a thought … what an image.

H: Yes, and here's another thought. I may come again to play some tricks on you! (*laughs*)

A: Please do. Some fun would be good. One last question: how can we know what is real and what is not?

H: You have to play the game without cheating. As a messenger of the gods, I could give you some helping hints, but that would take away from your own achievement. Even the gods have to achieve, you know. You must find that distinction for yourselves. I can say that you have everything you need, if you know where to look, and *how* to look.

And for the rest, well, you must discover your own achievements; otherwise, why be human?

A: Yes, indeed—why be human. Thank you, Hermes, for the chat.

H: You're most welcome. Remember that if you're going to play the game, then you should at least learn how to play the game well. Goodbye.

A: Goodbye.

Reflections

It seems as if many of us are playing games without realising that we are in the game itself. Nonetheless, many people are bent on cheating. What appear to be clever and "sophisticated" tactics are just childish, and many of us are absorbed by this child's play. As Hermes said, we were given a blank slate, and then we took out our pens and started scribbling everywhere. The mess is ours.

It's all in our heads. We invent these dramas, these boundary lines, and then we invest them with our crazy notions. We inherit the contradictions that run rampant in our minds. And we make them so real, and often so painful. There is a surrealism to what is going on here.

Our sandcastles and sand walls are fake, and they are going to come crashing down. We'll be left lying under our mountains of sand, and the weight of it all will continue to pile on top of us becoming increasingly heavier. That is, the weight is ours.

There must be a clearer way to see things—to cut through the fakery, the pen lines and the scribbles? Yet as Hermes rightly said, we cannot cheat on this. We've got to figure it all out for ourselves. And how easily we get caught out!

A tale

The student who caught a bird

A university student was taking a study break and sitting out in the gardens pondering on life, mathematics, and the universe—as students often do—when a pretty bird landed next to him. Without another ponderous thought the student reached out and in one fell swoop caught the bird up in his hand. Then something strange happened—the bird spoke …

It said: "A little bird like me is of no use to you, but if you will be kind enough to set me free, I will give you three pieces of advice."

The young student was amazed at his discovery. He listened further as the bird agreed to give the first piece of advice while still in his hand; the second while a few feet away on the grass; and the final piece while high on a branch above him. The student, thinking he would surely be the recipient of astounding advice agreed to this proposal.

The bird gave out the first piece of advice: "If you lose something, even if you value it as much as life itself—do not regret it."

The student, thinking on this first advice, let the bird go and it hopped to a few feet away on the grass, out of the student's reach. Then it gave the second piece of advice: "Never believe anything which is contrary to sense, without proof." And saying this it flew up to a branch on a nearby tree before the student had time to respond. And from this high branch the bird twittered with delight and called out to the student: "Oh, you poor daydreamer—if only you had killed me instead of listening to my chatter you would have found two large precious jewels inside me that would have made you a millionaire for life!"

The student gave out a wail of anguish and felt distressed at what he had just lost. After a few minutes the student managed to compose himself sufficiently to call out to the bird—"Well, at least give me my third piece of advice!"

"Ah, what a fool you are!" called back the bird. "You ask for more advice when you have not paid any heed to the first two pieces of advice given to you! I told you not to worry if you lose something, no matter how high you value it; and then never to believe anything which is contrary to sense. And you have done both. You are grieving because you think you have lost something which could have been yours. And secondly—look at me—I'm not big enough to carry two large jewels inside me! You have shown yourself to be a fool. Therefore, you must remain within your limited reality, a prisoner within the restrictions humankind places upon itself, for you are not yet ready to converse with the likes of me!"

And the little bird flew away, never to be seen again.

X

A chat with Mercury, Roman god of communication and deceit

Regarding this conversation, I had the idea to approach the subject of illusion. I didn't have anything specific to say or ask. Rather, it was a general issue on my mind since much of modern life seems predicated on it. Also, this theme had come up indirectly in previous chats. So, for this one I decided to reach out to Mercury, as he is the Roman god of deceit.

Author (A): Hello. I would like to make contact with Mercury, the Roman god of deceit. Can I speak with Mercury, please? Hello, Mercury?

Mercury (M): Greetings—you caught me just as I was passing through! (*chuckles*)

A: Great, glad to have caught you, I was …

M: Not caught! Certainly not caught—I meant I just happened to have been present, so you're lucky. You wouldn't have caught me if you'd tried, mind you.

A: Indeed. Yes, thank you. I'd just like a quick chat, if I may?

M: Sure, quick chat—go ahead.

A: Thanks. I wanted to ask you if you had anything to say about the nature of illusion, especially as it relates to us humans here on earth.

M: (*laughs*) Ah, now that's a topic or two! Illusion, yes, what a great topic. Is it here, or is it not? Is it real, or not? Aha, illusion has been one of the principal features for you humans. You thrive on it. You feed on it. It feeds on you! You think the sky is blue and the grass is green. You swear by it. Now that's an illusion!

A: Aren't they? I mean, isn't the sky blue and the grass green?

M: They're not from where I'm standing, but you humans have always insisted on *your* way of seeing, and everyone else's way is just plain wrong. You only see according to how your brain interprets things. Since you all have the same brainy things in your heads you all more or less see the same things. Sometimes a bump on the head is not a bad thing! (*laughs*)

A: So, everything is a matter of perception?

M: Sure it is. And you folks are all so gullible too. It's just so easy to fool you; as you say, to pull the wool over your eyes. You're easier to fool than the woolly mammoths, if you get my drift?

A: Certainly. And why do you think that is?

M: Well, it seems that whoever built you (*chuckles*) put in an in-built capacity for you to believe what you're told. I guess it made it easier to control you rowdy lot! But it's so true—you seem to believe whatever you hear or see. And especially if it comes from someone dressed as authority. You're all suckers for authority. All I have to do is come among you dressed in a uniform and you all get hypnotised. You don't use the inner faculty enough.

A: The inner faculty?

M: Yes. It's the faculty of true discernment that lies within you. You know, that voice of conscience and truth. That's also an in-built capacity but it hardly ever gets used. It's probably lying dormant, curled up in sleep. No wonder things are as they are with you all. You've stopped listening to yourselves. Now you just walk around listening to others. Well, listening to others if you're in a good mood. Most of the time you're not even listening at all. (*laughs*) I shake my head, I really do. That's what I'm doing right now.

A: Doing what?

M: Shaking my head. Like this.

A: Oh, I can't see anything.

M: No worries—one shake is as good as another.

A: Mm, right. Anyhow, do you think there are those who are deliberately trying to fool us?

M: Ah, for sure—open your eyes! Or better still, open your inner organ of discernment and listen carefully. There are so many things going on and yet you all seem to be in a daze.

A: You mean like in a trance?

M: Whoa, yeah, that's it! You're all tranced up. I really don't know where to begin trying to get messages through to you all. I mean, real messages, not with all the fakery that's going on. I do deliver real messages you know.

A: Really? And it's been that hard?

M: Sure, it has. It's no wonder why all us gods left you. You stopped listening to us a long time ago. Instead, you all turned back into your selfish gazes and went dumb and numb inside. You started to develop these systems of belief that told you that everything in the universe revolved around you. You started to believe that you were the masters!

A: Yes, maybe. We often refer to ourselves as "masters of our own fate".

M: There you go! But it's all just nonsense. You don't even know what this thing called "fate" actually is. Yet you use the word and pass it around as if it were a common article, like bread.

A: So, what is fate then?

M: (*sighs*) Here we go again. Your minds are easily diverted by curiosity. You like to collect bits of information to store it away and you call it knowledge. Your species is like a keeper of miscellaneous objects.

You are keepers of your own curiosity shop with thousands of things on display ... really ...

A: Yes, that sounds about right. So, no clarity on fate then?

M: Not likely. It's of no use to you right now. Whatever I told you would just be catalogued, filed, and stored away. You would not be able to *use* it. To return to the issue at hand—you are not masters of your fate. You are more like a *medium* for the life flow.

A: Life flow?

M: Yes. Life flows. It is an energy and a form of communication; a language, you could say. And it flows through you and into your world, your reality. Open yourself up to something that is more than you—that is *beyond* you—just for once.

A: Okay. And how do we start doing this?

M: Really? Well, you have to start listening. Maybe then some of us will slowly begin to come back. Meanwhile, we have other folks out there who need us. Speaking of that, I have a message I need to deliver. Got to go ... best of luck with it all—and get listening to yourselves!

A: Okay, thanks Mercury—good advice. Speedy travels. Bye.

Reflections

There we go again—the notion that we are full of our own illusions. We've opened up a deep, deep well and filled it to the top with all kinds of illusions; and then jumped into it with both feet. Well, it feels something like that. I liked the image that Mercury gave about the curiosity shop, and how we stock it with so much stuff. It's true, we store it all away without first taking the time—or learning how—to *process* it. It's somewhat akin to the magpie birds who are renowned for collecting—or rather stealing—shiny objects to take back to their nests. A bracelet here, a ring there; we notice that our shiny objects have gone missing. And somewhere there is a magpie nest that has these items tucked away. Yet the irony is that the magpie is unable to know how to use such items, nor even their value. They become like twigs and straw—just items to decorate the nest with.

Similarly, our minds so easily get diverted and distracted. We all like a shiny thing that grabs our attention. The modern world revolves around this. Much of life operates through the continual flow of shiny objects that we crave—from fashion to gold nuggets; from cars to diamonds and pearls. Or it can be as simple as what's on the TV. There is a lot of shiny stuff around; yet as the adage goes—not everything that glitters is gold.

A tale

The garden

There was a time when the art and science of gardening was not yet well established among humanity. At this time there existed a master gardener. Besides knowing the qualities of plants, their nutritional value, medicinal and aesthetic, the master gardener was granted knowledge of the herb of longevity and lived many hundreds of years. During these successive generations he visited gardens and cultivated places throughout the world. In each place where he planted a wonderful garden he would instruct the people to care for it and passed on his theory of gardening. However, as was the general pattern, many people would get used to seeing the plants growing and flourishing every year and would soon forget that some seeds had to be collected, that some others multiplied by cutting, others need greater abundance of water, and so on. The result was that over time such gardens became wild and the people began to believe that this was the best garden that could exist. After giving these people many opportunities to learn gardening, the master gardener would have to train others in the art of gardening in some other location. He warned that if not looked after correctly then the garden would deteriorate, and all would suffer. Yet each group in turn would gradually forget, and because they were lazy they cared only for fruits and flowers that were easy to cultivate and left the others to die. From time to time there came a few others who, having successfully learned from the master gardener before, would offer advice and tell others they "must do this and that". But they were pushed away by shouts of— "You are the ones that are far from the truth in this matter!"

The master gardener persisted to cultivate other gardens, but none was perfect, except those that he attended to with his top helpers. When it was learned that there were many gardens and even gardening methods, people started going to visit various gardens, to make comparisons, to criticise, or to argue about them.

Some wrote books about the subject, gardening assemblies were established, gardening topics were placed in categories according to what they thought was the correct order of priority.

As is common among people, the difficulty is that gardeners are too easily attracted by superficiality. They say: "I like this flower," and want everyone else to like it too; and, despite its attractiveness or wealth, it can be a weed that is strangling other plants, which may provide medicine or food that people and the garden need for support and retention. Among these people are those who prefer plants of a single colour; these are described as "good". There are others who only care for the plants and refuse to deal with the beds or borders.

When at last the old master gardener died he left behind a legacy of the full knowledge of gardening; it was distributed among those people who understood, according to their capabilities. Thus, both the science and art of gardening as an inheritance has been scattered in many gardens, and various reports have been made about them. People who often begin to learn of gardening find it difficult to understand the subtleties needed to nurture the right balance of growth. Often such people begin to judge, criticise, reject, or imagine what they think to be needed for a garden. Yet from time to time true gardeners arise. Such is the abundance of semi-gardens, that when people hear about a real garden they are likely to say, "Oh yes! You speak of a garden as we have or imagine." However, the real experts, who cannot reason with pseudo-gardeners, continue to work to maintain the vitality and presence of real gardens throughout the world.

The others, the pseudo-gardeners, are often forced to dress up so as to appeal to the imaginations of the people who want to learn with them. Yet at such gatherings we can hear the questions—"How can I get the most beautiful flowers from these onions?" True gardeners, however, continue to work with the people they can in order to raise real gardens for the benefit of humankind.

XI

A chat with Saraswati, Hindu goddess of knowledge, music, arts, wisdom, and learning

My first thought on approaching this next conversation was on the commodity of art, and how some of the finer things in life can be treated, or boxed, into such crude forms. To get a better perspective on this I decided to call upon the Hindu goddess Saraswati.

Author (A): Hello Saraswati. Are you available for a chat? I would like to speak with Saraswati.

Saraswati (S): (*sounds of soft music*) Hello!

A: Hello Saraswati. It is indeed an honour to speak with you.

S: Greetings and blessings upon you.

A: Thank you. I wonder if you may honour me with a brief chat?

S: Words and speech are what I bring to your world, among many other gifts that are your inheritance. Of course—speak on!

A: Thank you. I notice that you bring so many gifts, such as learning, music, and the arts. These are indeed wonders for our world. And yet sometimes I get to wondering why it is that so many of these gifts are misused or diluted into trivial forms. Does this not displease you?

S: (*giggles*) Perhaps you do not know your own world as well as we do. What you speak of is expected to be the case. Not every seed that is planted comes to fruition. So many seeds are planted in the knowledge that a few of them will find their roots and grow into wondrous delights.

A: So, you are aware of how some of the arts are being commoditised and trivialised in our cultures?

S: Yes, of course. This is also the nature of your world. It is a dense realm, and the finer substances that enter will also become dense and crystallised with time. That is why knowledge and learning, and knowledge of the arts, are constantly updated. Nothing stays still in your realm. Music must keep flowing, following the rivers of adaptation and mutation that pass on their learning and mastery to each upward flow. Some of this flow of learning gets trapped at the side of the river; this is the silt that falls as sediment and which at times blocks and hinders the flow. Yet eventually the flow will win out, for it is carried along with a stronger force. The sediment will get absorbed into your terrestrial earth and become recycled, and again it will attempt to move along with the river towards its rightful destination.

A: So, you are saying that the flow of the arts and learning will continue throughout our world, despite the solidifications that we see.

S: This is indeed the case—it always has been and will always be. Many of your human institutions focus solely upon the heavy sediments of culture and learning, and not upon the lightness of its flow. Often your focus is upon the mortal remains, the traces that only hint at the wonders of wisdom. As a species you are beguiled and enamoured by the heavy, dirty things. Seek out the lightness; seek to immerse yourselves in the flow.

A: Yes, I understand this. And yet the heavy, coarse aspects of the arts are the things which are thrust upon us. Many people find it hard to escape this world of the dense matter that surrounds us all the time.

S: This is your own excuse. The world of permanent wisdom flows through you and your world ceaselessly. All you need is to give it your proper attention. There is laziness in many of you upon your world, and this makes you turn away from the wonders. All you need to do is learn how to see. Over time you have closed down your senses. Your window onto reality is so small it only allows in a slither of sunlight and spirit. Imagine yourself in your own home. If you are looking through a small window you will only see a small percentage of what lies outside. You have done the same with your senses of reality. And within this short spectrum you see more of the dense, solidified forms, and less of the lightness.

A: We need to open our senses then?

S: This and much more. It is not only about being open. You need also to be aware.

A: Could you explain the difference here?

S: If you are open you see more things. Yet without awareness you are unable to understand what you see. It is like seeing a shape far in the distance. You know something is there, but you are unable to make it out. Without this perception you cannot know its function, or what you must do. You are seeing, but you are helpless. Once you begin to be open, to allow your senses to perceive, you then need to develop your awareness.

A: I understand what you are saying, in theory. But how can we develop this awareness?

S: First you need to clean yourselves out. (*giggles*) You are so cluttered inside.

A: With things?

S: (*laughs*) With thoughts! Your ideas, beliefs, and everything. You surround yourselves with filters. You grow up building your filters around you. Wisdom is about knowing how to let go. Knowledge is a river and wisdom are the waters that flow through it. If the rivers become blocked, then the waters cannot flow. Your beliefs are like the rocks and branches that fall into the river and disrupt the flow of the water. They are obstacles. And your fixed ideas become the obstacles within you.

A: Yes, that makes sense.

S: Oh, wise you! (*giggles*) You are surrounded by many waters and you can choose within which one you wish to swim. Do not blame others for your own choices.

A: Thank you—that is uplifting news.

S: You can be uplifted and carried by the flow at all times, despite the severity of your circumstances. Never forget the capacity to choose. Wisdom is like the music of the spheres. It is ever flowing. Your cosmos is built upon music. Consider this and you shall learn much. Now, choose wisely in your steps. I leave you here. I cannot stay much longer. I am being carried away. Place your awareness within the flow, dear one. Blessings to you.

A: Blessings and goodbye.

Reflections

The issue is less about external objects themselves and more about our own awareness. Of course, there is commodification and strong material aspects to our world; yet it's as much about the attention that we choose to place upon them. It's as if we make these things denser by placing more focus and attention upon them; or rather, the incorrect form of attention. If we are attracted to something, such as some art, then we should ask ourselves why this is so. In other words, we can observe—be aware—of our own forms of attention. What I feel Saraswati is saying here is that humans have a tendency to project outwards, not realising that the source comes from within. The result is that it is *we* who block the flow. We should perhaps step back and allow this flow to continue on its way.

It can be so difficult to accept that we need to let go—or even to know how to begin to let go. It is easy to have so many feelings and ideas about what needs to be done and yet it is harder to act upon this intuitive knowing. Again, preferring to rely upon the external senses—what we can see and touch, etc.—rather than our inner feelings. In this, we lose a great portion of our innate perception.

As individuals, we block the flow of life through our rigid thoughts, opinions, and inculcated values that cling to us as baggage. Such things make it harder to cross the river to reach the other side.

A tale

A river to cross

One particularly fine spring day two men of faith were out taking a good long walk through the hills and ravines close to their retreat. The elder of the two was a well-respected man of piety and morality who had served his community for many years. The younger man regarded the elder as his mentor and role model. The two men were also good friends and often enjoyed their company together. On this occasion, as on many others, the two friends were sharing stories and articles of their faith.

Later that morning, during the course of their walk together, they came upon a shallow river that blocked their path. It was then that they noticed, under a tree by the side of the river, a young, attractive woman with her head in her hands. Upon seeing the two men approach the young woman sprang to her feet in obvious relief and pleaded with them to help her across the river.

"The water is shallow, this I know," said the young woman notably distraught. "Yet I have a terrible fear of water from an unpleasant experience I had as a young child. Please, you must help me across—it is imperative I reach my destination across the other side by lunchtime." The young man listened to her pleas yet was moved not. Instead, he distrustfully eyed the young woman, her scantily clad attire and her suspicious demeanour.

"For my part, I cannot," said the young man, "for it is unseemly for a man of my faith to be in close contact with such ... such a one as you. You must walk across the river by yourself." The young man proceeded to wade across the shallow river as the young woman wept. The young man, proud in his adherence to discipline, expected the older man to follow him across the river. Yet when he looked behind, he saw, to his horror and disbelief, the old man shamelessly pick up the young lady and carry her in his arms. The young woman, in fear of the water, pressed her body close to the old man and clung to him tightly. When the old man had reached the other side, he carefully put the woman down and, without another word, continued on his way.

The young man, stammering, soon marched off close behind him. The young man did not know what to say, so shocked had he been by what he saw. He walked alongside the older man in silence yet inside he was fuming. He had respected and looked up to the older man for so many years. He had considered him his mentor, a role model in piety. Had he, after all these years, been wrong in his respect for this man? Was he just a fake? A false man of faith? A hypocrite? The young man was tormented by these thoughts and yet he did not know how to approach the older man or how to broach his concerns to him.

At noontime the older man sat under a tree and spread out a small picnic he had prepared and offered it to share. The young man ate in silence, his inner world in turmoil and gripped by doubt. After their lunch the two men continued their walk in silence and by dusk they had returned to their retreat. As the older man was about to say goodnight and retire for the evening he turned to his younger friend and said, "You have been wishing to speak with me on a certain matter all day and yet have kept silent. Now is the time to speak—I am listening."

The young man poured out his grievances and his disbelief at the older man's actions. It was, he said, an act against the cleanliness of their faith, to be in intimate contact with such … such a woman of her calling. When the younger man had finally finished his outburst, the older man turned to him calmly and said, in a steady voice:

"I picked up that woman and carried her to the other side of the river. And then I put her down. But you, ***you are still carrying her!****"*

XII

A chat with Morpheus, Greek god of dreams

Dreams have fascinated me since childhood. I have always considered them as having importance, even when they may seem illogical or surreal. Also, the notion of collective dreaming interests me since we are often told that humanity is asleep! So, for this conversation I decided to approach Morpheus, the Greek god of dreams, with a little trepidation.

Author (A): Hello, hello Morpheus, are you there? I would like to speak with you.

(*a low moan*)

Author (A): Hello Morpheus—is that you?

Morpheus (M): I guess that depends on which "you" you are referring to.

A: Sorry, but I always half expect someone else to turn up. Each time it's always a pleasant surprise.

M: (*low chuckle*) How human of you! Always a pleasant surprise you say. Well, I am Morpheus, and I hope you find me a pleasant surprise to your liking.

A: Hello Morpheus. It is a pleasure indeed. And thank you for turning up for this quick chat.

M: Not a problem, I was just in the neighbourhood—as you earthlings like to say. Besides, I can be here and many other places simultaneously so it's not a bother; unless you bore me, that is.

A: Well, I certainly hope I won't be boring you. And since you are the god of dreams, you're just the person I wish to speak with.

M: And how's that? And am I a "person"? Anyway, tell me more before you forget. Are you going to request me to enter into someone's dreams to influence them? This is what I normally get asked for by humans. They pray and beg me to enter into the dreams of someone they know, which is usually their loved one. (*chuckle*) Ah, humans are nothing if not predictable! So, tell me, do you have someone whom you'd like me to make fall in love with you?

A: Well, yes and no. But that's not the point, and it's not why I'm here. I wish to speak about our collective dreams, as a species.

M: Ah, you wish to enquire over the bigger picture, the bigger dream. Yes, that's the one you least suspect, and which influences your species the most. All of your civilisations have been born from collective dreaming, in one way or another.

A: That's what I suspected. Perhaps you could say a little of how this works?

M: I could, yet there is only so much I can tell you. I'm not wishing to be rude, but your species has not yet arrived at the place where, by its own free will, it can receive and understand all that there is to know. Information comes according to your capacity to receive and understand it. If I tell you something that is beyond the remit of your capacity, it may in fact hinder you or confuse you.

A: Can you tell me *something*?

M: Yes, I can tell you something; and I shall, for it is permitted at this time. I say permitted because we have seen the potentials of your species on this planet at this time, and you have made a step towards your next phase of evolution. Soon much more information will be released to you; for now, I shall share a little.

A: Thanks.

M: There is a collective dream of the species, as you call it. Yet it does not belong solely to yourselves. It is shared by all, including other species on your planet as well as the planet itself. Although we can call it a "collective dream", in truth this is not accurate. It is more like an information field. And all things on your planet are a part of this information field. And sentient creatures, such as yourselves, can both receive and transmit into this field. During your sleep state you are active within this field, receiving more than transmitting.

A: And this is where we get our dreams from—our ideas and our inspirations?

M: Correct. And through this field humanity is provided information and knowledge that guides you. You do not need to be sleeping in order to receive information from this field. It is continually communicating with you, beyond your awareness. By being alive you are participating within this field. It is a living intelligence. *It* doesn't dream as it is always awake. It is the human species who are dreaming, living their lives half awake. The more you awaken, the more you will consciously receive and understand this living intelligence field.

A: And are we continually transmitting back into this field?

M: Correct. That is so. The minds of humanity are also feeding back into this field, for better or for worse.

A: Why do you say for worse?

M: I say that because your thought forms also influence the collective field, which in turn affects the energy of your planet. Disruptive, angry, chaotic thought forms add to the potential disharmony of the planet's energetic alignment. What you dream indeed comes to fruition, in one way or another. And you do not need to be asleep for this to function. Each of your thoughts, your emotions, in every moment, they fold back into this living intelligence field. Individually this is not such an issue. It is when you collectively share a particular thought form, such as a powerful emotion or trauma. If this is shared among many of you then there is a disturbance in the collective field. Dreams interact both ways.

A: And so, the Muses really do exist?

M: (*low chuckle*) Yes, they do. They form part of the potentials in this field of dreams, if you will. What inspires you comes from this communication.

A: And you say that we have taken a step forward in our evolution. Does this mean we are soon going to exit our current period of transition? I have often referred to these transition years as bringing temporary disruption.

M: You *will* exit these tumultuous years. However, exactly *how* will be down to your own making. This is all a part of your collective free will. Yet the potentials are there. As you often like to say—it is only a matter of time.

A: And are we really waking up, as a species?

M: Yes, of course, and you were always meant to. Yet do not get too excited, it is not an overnight thing. You must think in terms of generations.

A: Sure, I suspected that. One last question: has the collective field been responsible for leaving signs and guidance within our cultures, for our awakening?

M: Yes and no. It is not as simple as that. There has been guidance and teachings, of course, from the very beginning. Many of these signs do originate from the living intelligence field of which I have spoken. Yet there are also such "signs"—as you call them—that are placed intentionally within your cultures by those who live and operate within your cultures.

A: This is interesting. And who are these people, these "operatives"—can you tell me more?

M: I can tell you no more than you already know or suspect. Many of these "operatives", as you say, have been known to you throughout history. And many more have not. Those you know, you know; and those you don't, you don't. I can say no more than this. You have been capable of receiving this information. More will come as you proceed. So, don't forget to keep dreaming; it seems to be a favourite human pastime. (*laughs*)

A: Indeed, we should never forget to dream. But at the same time, we must be awake, right?

M: That is so. A pleasant conundrum, you might say. May it please you, and may it take you forward. Keep awake in your dreams. And now I feel it is time to leave.

A: Thank you, Morpheus. It has been a pleasure. Goodbye.

M: So long, for now …

Reflections

Dreams within dreams, like the layers of a Matryoshka Russian doll. We often consider dreaming to be a negative thing, such as calling a person a "daydreamer". Dreams have often been regarded culturally as wishy-washy things that idle or distracted minds engage in. Yet dreams are much more solid and real than this. Dreams are not just some bunch of flickering images (although they can be this too), but can act as a kind of transmission of information.

One individual mind may have its dreams and/or its preoccupations; many minds may dip in and out of a collective storyline. Perhaps we are all players in this grand story narrative, and each of us is adding our own thread to the story arc. It is similar to an author group who collaborate together, taking turns to add to the ongoing story.

Yet what comes in also goes out. It's a two-way traffic. Many wisdom traditions have cautioned us to watch our thoughts; to be alert to negative thinking. As Shakespeare famously said: *"All the world's a stage …"* and maybe, just maybe, the world story as it gets played out is but the thought-forms manifesting from the human collective dream.

We can dream harder, yet we should also be aware that in dreams begin responsibilities. Otherwise, we may get caught up in someone else's dream.

A tale

The VIP dinner

There was once a well-known television stage magician and hypnotist who amassed great wealth from his regular appearances in the media. Soon he decided to build for himself a large house near a well-to-do and prosperous village. When the house was finished, he invited all the people of the village to dinner. The locals were all very excited and were much looking forward to meeting their famous host. They all arrived in their best clothes and jewellery hanging from their arms.

The famous television host appeared and said: "Before we eat, we have some entertainments."

Everyone was thrilled and pleased, and the magician host provided a first-class conjuring show, with rabbits coming out of hats, flags appearing from nowhere, and one thing turning into another. The people were delighted. Then their host asked: "Would you like dinner now, or more entertainments?"

Everyone called for more entertainments, for they had never seen anything like it before; at home there was food, but never such excitement as this. So the famous hypnotist changed himself into a pigeon, then into a hawk, and finally into a phoenix that rose from the ashes. The people went wild with excitement.

He asked them again, and they wanted more. And so, they got more entertainment. Finally, he asked them if they wanted to eat, and they said that they did. So, their hypnotist host made them feel that they were eating, diverting their attention with a number of tricks, through his deceptive powers.

The imaginary eating and entertainments went on all night. When it was dawn, some of the people said, "We must go to work." The host made those people imagine that they went home, got ready for work, and actually did a day's work.

In short, whenever anyone said that they had to do something, the host made them think first that they were going to do it, then, that they had done it, and finally that they had come back to the stage magician's house.

Eventually, the host had woven such spells over the people of the village that they worked only for him while they thought that they were carrying on with their ordinary lives. Whenever they felt a little restless he made them think that they were back at dinner at his house, and this gave them pleasure and made them forget.

And what happened to the magician and the people in the end? Do you know, I cannot tell you, because he is still busily doing it, and the people are still largely under his spell.

XIII

A chat with Demeter, Greek goddess of the harvest and agriculture, and of natural cycles

We live our lives through the ongoing seasons, which show us the ebb and flow, the birth and decay, that fill our lives. These are the natural cycles. For this next conversation I wanted to ask about these cycles, and whether they are changing. For this, I decided to call upon Demeter, the Greek goddess that is associated with natural cycles.

Author (A): Hello, I would like to begin a conversation with the Greek goddess Demeter. Demeter, are you there? Hello?

Demeter (D): Greetings. Yes, I am here.

A: Thank you. May we speak?

D: Yes, of course. Although I'm always very busy, I'm also available for moments like these. It's all about balance and putting spaces in the flow of cycles. Without these spaces there would be no true rhythm.

A: Thanks. Yes, I wanted to talk about cycles and how they operate.

D: Well, let me begin by saying that cycles don't come back on themselves the same as when they began. Nothing repeats itself exactly the same.

Otherwise, there would be no change. Cycles are actually about moving forward, and not about going around and around on the same spot, as many may think.

A: I see. Does that mean we are talking more about spirals then?

D: In a sense this is so; yet it is also a limiting formulation. Try not to pin these things down. Humans are always trying to do this—to pin something down in order to observe it and make an entry in their archive. Like the way some of your collectors pin their butterflies down and stick them in glass cases. The result is that you end up observing a dead thing. Cycles can be spirals, of course. Yet this is only according to a particular dimensional perspective. What cycles are actually about is not shape but movements.

A: Okay, I think I can get that. Can you tell me something about these movements?

D: Yes, I can. Movements are about allowing things to manifest and to play out through formations and patterns. Or, to better put it into your words—allowing things to happen. Happenings participate in the fabric of creation and make connections. They allow connections to happen, which in turn allow creative processes to manifest. These processes are sometimes what you humans have poetically referred to as the "movement of the heavens".

A: Thank you. You talk about creative processes, and yet these movements, or cycles, deal in death also. Is this a creative process?

D: Why—of course! Here again we arrive at the misconceptions of your general thinking. It shows that there is a tendency between humans to see things as separate boxes lined up in a linear fashion. This is my box, here. This is yours, there. And everything has its own box. It seems to us more like a streak of childlike possession. You see, you have "life" in this box here, which is the "good box" by the way (*laughs*); and death is placed over in the corner as the "bad box". Yet you see, life and death are happenings that form a part of the same movement, if that makes sense?'

A: Yes, I think it does. It's like one influences the other, and one also needs the other. Right?

D: Neat, but not quite! Again, can't you see how you have separated these into two factions? You said "one" here and the "one" there influence each other. The only thing correct you have said here is the word "one".

A: How do you mean?

D: What I mean is that they are "one". They are the same thing. Life is death and death is life. They are not separate things. As you are living you are also dying. And in dying you are also living. Why do you have to see everything so categorically divided?

A: Maybe as a result of my early maths training?

D: (*laughs*) Blame it on the maths! Don't you feel like a naughty schoolchild?

A: Okay, okay—you got me! Alright, I was trying to be funny.

D: Please don't. You're only confusing things by hiding in this way.

A: Yes, you are right. Please, can you go on?

D: Of course. Now look, everything is coming in and out of formation. Take your own body for example. As your body continues to grow and develop it relies on the continual dying of your cells. Your cells are constantly being replaced. If not, your whole body would stagnate and cease functioning. In this example, your body needs elements of what you call "death" to occur in order to maintain "life". They are aspects of the same thing.

A: Ah, now that makes sense. And what about Nature, is it the same here?

D: Of course, it is: why would it be separate? You observe the seasons shifting in your world and you consider that one thing dies over what you call "winter", and another may be born in "spring". Each season you have placed into a box. Some regions have four season boxes, others two. Oh, how neat the boxes! So, tell me, on what dates do these seasons begin and end?

A: Well, erh—it's not as simple as that. They don't start on any one day. Rather, they start and end over a period of time. And this may vary each year.

D: In your perspective maybe; and you can keep your perspective to yourself, it's faulty! (*laughs*) That's right. It's not as simple as that. Life and death, as you call it, is one thing: it is unified and complete. And it is going through a process. This process of movement is what you perceive as cycles within your constructs of time.

A: And therefore, when we see death occurring, it is also a manifestation of life?

D: Now you're starting to get it. When something in your reality moves out of formation, or manifestation, it allows other forms to emerge. Nothing disappears. You have a law in your world that recognises this; it goes something like energy can neither be created nor destroyed. This is a correspondence that also manifests in cycles, or spirals, or however you wish to see the movement. Energy is coming in and out of formation, and each movement is assisting another. No start or stop.

A: No boxes?

D: (*laughs*) No boxes!

A: And are these cycles changing now, upon our planet?

D: Yes, they are. And why shouldn't they be?

A: Well, I was thinking specifically about human intervention. Whether we had caused any recent changes to occur?

D: Oh yes, of course. The big humans have changed everything—the universe revolves around them. Here we go again! Now, listen here. Yes, you do influence things. Of course you do, for you are part of the whole fabric. Yet you are not influencing your world and its cycles in the ways you think you are. It's not a question of A, B, C, or one thing leads to another thing. Cycles as you perceive them are shifting because there are other movements coming into play. Everything within the whole fabric of what you consider simply as "Life" is in constant motion. Yet you cannot see this because you choose not to consciously participate. Most of the time you move along as driftwood. Isn't that a shame—a species that exists as driftwood? So, you see, you need to perceive the grander movements and rhythms by learning to participate in them. Get yourself out of your human boxes.

A: We're in our own containment box, right?

D: Of course you are! You've boxed yourselves in. It's now time to open the lid and come on out.

A: Time to dance with the cycles?

D: Dance with the harvests like you used to do, remember?

A: Ah, yes, we used to do the harvest dances.

D: Well then, start to dance again. Yet this time through your awareness and your hearts—not just your legs! (*laughs*)

A: Thanks, Demeter. I appreciate that.

D: Well, glad it helped. I'm off now. I have some other type of harvesting to do.

A: Okay, thanks a lot. Bye, Demeter.

D: Byeee …

Reflections

The conversation made me feel like I was living in a house that had been prepared for moving. It was full of boxes everywhere. All my stuff stored in boxes and I wasn't sure where I had put things. You know that feeling, when you have to rummage through various boxes to try to find that item you had packed away somewhere? Maybe that's how the inside of our brains look. Well, not all brains … but enough of them.

Death is a delicate subject. It is both a necessary subject and yet oddly taboo in modern, Western society. In fact, we often deliberately try to avoid discussing it. We have been conditioned to find it uncomfortable; or we don't have the right words to deal with it or express it. We often struggle to know what to say around death. That's why we often recite poems or song lyrics at funerals, because somehow, they express it better for us.

Yet all is one thing—all is in movement. This is reassuring, as well as needing time to fully digest. I feel that within us we can all resonate with this as it makes sense. The problem, however, is in trying to make it a living concept for us.

The analogy of the body is a good one: in order to live a little more, we need to die a little more, each day. The process is a unified one, and everything works together in collaboration. This is a good way to think about it. Everything has its natural place and function, which we should not try to avoid.

A tale

When death came to hollywood

One afternoon a well-known movie producer in Hollywood was taking a break and having coffee in a downtown coffee shop. As this producer was famous in the movie world, but more so because he disliked having to deal with people socially, he snuck himself into a small corner table with his beret lowered over his face. He tried not to notice as two figures came to sit down at the table next to him.

Yet as they began talking the producer could not help but overhear. And he soon realised, after listening for a few minutes, that one of the figures was none other than the Angel of Death. He should know, after all, since one of his favourite films was Ingmar Bergman's The Seventh Seal.

"I have several calls to make in this city over the next couple of weeks," said the Angel of Death to his unidentified companion.

Terrified of the prospect of death being in the city the producer quickly had a plan. Using his cunning, which he was well-known for, he came up with a strategy to make sure he could cheat a possible call from death. He would make himself scarce for at least the next two weeks and get out of the city. The producer left the coffee shop as fast as he could and jumped into his expensive car. Without even bothering to pack anything he headed straight to Nevada and to Las Vegas. If he was going to hide out for a couple of weeks then at least it would be in style, he reasoned.

Meanwhile, a short time later the Angel of Death went to visit one of his acquaintances for a chat, a top director in Hollywood, to whom Death had, in the past, provided several story ideas. "And where is your best producer, the one who's always here?" asked Death.

"He should be back soon," replied the director. "He just stepped out to get a coffee."

"Surprising," said the Angel of Death, "because I have him on my list. Let me see, yes, here he is. It says I have a meeting with him shortly in Las Vegas—would you believe it?"

XIV

A chat with Abraxos, Pagan god of duality

In considering how there are many forms of division and separation in our lives, which we see as a construct of duality, this is likely to be a result of how humans perceive the world. Regarding this subject, I wasn't initially sure whom to approach to ask on this. Finally, I opted for the Pagan god Abraxos as this unusual deity has been associated with the nature of duality. I was more apprehensive than usual, as the lineage of this deity is varied and controversial.

Author (A): Is Abraxas there? Is Abraxas available for a chat? (*pause*) Hello?

Abraxas (Ab): Who calls?

A: Hello. I would like to speak with Abraxas.

Ab: Well, you're certainly not the first. And you won't be the last. So, go on. What is it?

A: Thank you. I know there is some confusion over your identity. You have been named as a Gnostic deity, an Egyptian, and also related with Hebrew and Greek traditions. You've even been recognised as a demon.

Ab: Well, that's your problem. What do you wish me to do about it?

A: Nothing. That's not the point. I don't wish to get into this debate here. I'm not concerned with how you've been labelled.

Ab: Good—that makes two of us then! Ah, now that's a duality. (*low chuckle*) Yes, yes. It's all about your divisions. Your religions, your paths, your dogmas, your "expertise" knowledge ... really. And when you run out of ideas, then you come up with the demon. As usual, it says everything about yourselves and almost nothing about me.

A: And who are you then?

Ab: That's not the issue here. I know who I am. If you don't know, then that's your problem. Let me just say that in your linear terms of time I am very old. I'm totally antiquated! I was present in the old minds of your species. The old minds were simpler. They perceived things in greater clarity because there was less mental pollution. Such minds did not differentiate a great deal. There was less intellectual component, as you call it. More primeval and instinctual. There was more wholeness. I worked with such minds and it was easier. This is a long time back in your human history. Later peoples have tagged me with various allegiances. You could say I am all of them—and yet none.

A: And yet you have become known as representing duality. Perhaps this is the demonic side of you?

Ab: The demons are within your own minds. This is truer than you may realise. Reflect on this before you begin to project it upon others. You can say that one aspect of Abraxas is the nature of duality, because your dual, or rather fragmented minds, forced this upon me.

A: Ah, so your duality is a reflection of our fragmented minds?

Ab: Sure, like everything is. Didn't the other so-called deities tell you this?

A: Not in so many words.

Ab: Ha! (*laughs*) Not in so many words. Here we go again. You are back to your languages and your tongue-confusion. Look here, you are only able to grasp according to your ability to understand. When you get more perception, more understanding will open up to you. You're still struggling for air, as you often say, while in your split minds.

A: And how are our minds split?

Ab: They're split because they are disconnected from your environment. And I don't mean just the natural environment. I mean your reality environment. Since a long time ago, your species has considered itself separate from your reality-structure.

A: Reality-structure?

Ab: Okay, I think I need to be simpler here. Let's say, that which you call "your" cosmos. You perceive one thing as outside, and the other as inside. Up there in the skies you have the cosmos with the starry heavens, or however you like to call it in your vernacular. Then the "down here" is a planet of rock with a few walking biped brains upon it. There's the "out there" and the "in here". What you receive is what's been dealt to you by the "out there". When it's not in your favour you demonise it. When it helps, you anglicise it. Either way, you separate off into two divisions. Within these divisions you have further separations and splits. The end result is a fragmented understanding of reality and the world. Your perceiving apparatus is like a broken mirror and you are seeing each part reflected in one of its broken shards. You exist in this shattered hall of mirrors. When you see whole, you perceive from a complete, coherent mirror. Then the true reflection you see will be a reflection of yourselves. And this is how it is.

A: And why did we end up with this fragmented mind, or perception?

Ab: Part of it was your coping mechanism. It helped you to focus on your survival and immediate needs. Then this got locked in, and you further reinforced it. There were some other factors beyond your control. Let's call them cosmic factors.

A: Cosmic factors—how do you mean?

Ab: Well, without getting into details, or making this more complex than it needs to be, there was a break in the connection, temporarily. Let's say the phone line went down briefly. When this happened, your brains scrambled for more local, immediate connections. You were expected to connect up with the planet more. To get into a kind of resonance, as you say.

A: But we didn't?

Ab: It's not that you didn't. It's more that you did so in your own ways, and not as expected. You did focus on the planet's environment, but you increasingly saw yourselves as separate from it. Perhaps you went into a kind of panic attack. Unconsciously, you sensed a break in the larger connection, and feeling alone all of a sudden you went into withdrawn survival mode. Everything became your enemy, more or less. And this included your natural environment. You fell into a state of duality.

A: This was our Fall?

Ab: Say it how you wish. I don't want you to start mythologising everything. But more or less, yes. And we've been trying to get you all back on the line ever since. Get it now?

A: Yes, I think so. It does sort of make sense.

Ab: Maybe that's good enough, for now!

A: And so, it's crucial that we now collectively break free from this perception of duality. We need to re-whole our fragmented minds, right?

Ab: Sure thing, genius! (*low chuckle*) You've all got some rewiring to do. Yet it's begun. It's coming along.

A: Could you say more about this rewiring?

Ab: Mm. I could, yet I won't. Saying more might only hinder it at this stage. There are forces coming in that will push you in the required directions. You will adapt—or you won't. That's all I'm saying. Call me a demon if you like!

A: Okay, thank you Abraxas. That's all been useful.

Ab: Make of it what you can. But just don't build a religion around it! I'm off. Keep it together.

A: Sure, Abraxas. Thanks.

Ab: Yup. See you around—maybe.

Reflections

If our minds are split, then everything we see and filter through our understanding will be divided too. I guess that's the bottom line. The question is though, what can we do about it? Seeing everything as outside ourselves has been a handy survival strategy. It's also been a way of excusing ourselves from our actions. And it has been responsible for hiding the bigger picture from us. It's like we've placed ourselves into a mental quarantine and we can't find the exit door, or the door beyond.

It seems as if in these current times the social and cultural divisions are getting wider again. And national issues are mounting and coming back into the forefront. We are seeing this also within our political systems, especially those that play upon the divisions and the fear they create around this. This only serves to strengthen the divided mind. And this, in turn, leads to increased social and cultural fragmentation. We are the source of this issue. We literally need to change *how we think*.

A divided self will only lead to a divided world. I think the shattered mirror was a good analogy here. We are looking out at the world through splintered shards. It is a form of self-delusion—or self-hypnosis.

A tale

Another day at the office

There is a story which has existed in one form or another for as long as there have been human beings. The style of its telling changes with the time and place in which it is shared. In our day it begins with a very rich man who was the boss of a large company. As well as being rich he was also very mean, both in terms of his money as well as his behaviour towards others. He was so mean that he didn't want to hire supervisors to look after his employees, and instead expected his employees to get on with their jobs and to work all hours of every day. Of course, as is the way of people, the employees would often call in sick, take long breaks, and become distracted at work with chatting on social media with their friends. Eventually the boss became frustrated that his company was not performing as well as it should. Finally, the mean boss came up with a solution.

He found a magician who, for a little persuasion, was willing to hypnotise his employees. And so, the boss had all his employees hypnotised to believe that what they were doing was of great importance to the world and it gave them also much personal satisfaction. He also suggested to them that the meagre salary they were receiving was more than enough because they could apply for credit to buy all the things necessary for a comfortable life, such as a new television, a car, the latest smartphone and other gadgets, etc.

He also suggested to his employees that he was a good boss and that they should work hard for him, and not take any time off because any laziness would be an insult to the world that took care of them. To work hard to the very end of their lives, in fact, was a virtuous quality that made them "good people". And finally, for good measure, he decided to suggest to a few of his employees that they were better than the others, and deserved respect from their peers. And to some others he suggested that they needed to prove they were better than the others. In this way, he ensured that there would be enough personal rivalry and friction to keep his employees in competition among themselves.

And after that, as you can imagine, the mean boss had very few, if any, problems with his employees. But that didn't stop him from continuing to dislike them all!

XV

A chat with Athena, Greek goddess of wisdom, handicrafts, and war

For this next chat I was thinking about the nature of the human struggle, and how this has often been seen in terms of conflict. Why do we struggle so much? For this conversation, I decided to call upon Athena, the Greek goddess known for her protection and patronage of heroes.

Author (A): Hello, Athena—are you there? Can we talk? Are you available?

Athena (At): Hello?

A: Hello, Athena. Is it okay if we have a chat?

At: Sure. What's on your mind?

A: Well, I was thinking about how humans always appear to be struggling. It seems that the nature of struggle is built into us as a species. You must have seen this a lot, especially in terms of warfare?

At: Where there is warfare there can also be found wisdom. Nothing comes in isolation. Yes, I have witnessed a great deal of what you refer to as human struggle. It comes in many forms. This does not need to be seen only as a negative thing. When you say struggle, consider also courage, determination, nobility, strength, and yes—wisdom. Struggle is often a healthy and necessary quality.

A: Necessary? What do you mean by this?

At: The power and force of struggle is required in order to achieve change and progress. Things move forward because there has been a *need* for them. It is this journey towards necessity that has defined much of the successes of your species. Do not forget this.

A: That's a good point. Can you say more about these achievements?

At: I can say a great deal. I will limit myself here, though. Yet consider that it is important to have incentive, to have a goal to acquire. This has been the manifestation of what you can consider as the evolutionary drive. By this, I refer to the inner drive, not those you consider as external, environmental forces. They exist too, of course. Yet there is an evolutionary necessity that exists within the inner core of the human being. And this striving has often been expressed through the outward human struggle. That is why many such acts of fortitude have been depicted as journeys, or quests. For this is what they are—they are a quest.

A: That's interesting, Athena. We could say then that we have arrived here, collectively as a species, through these many quests.

At: Indeed, you have. Many of these emblematic quests were undertaken by a few, or by an individual. These are the heroic quests that become also your myths and fables. They portray the traits of nobility, perseverance, fortitude, and self-belief that were necessary to convey to your peoples and to seed into your societies and cultures.

A: So, were these quests real or fables?

At: They were both. We see no distinction. Of course, many quests were actual physical ones; that is, real, as you say. Others were symbolic quests that also served a similar purpose in portraying a pattern for your species' collective mind. For are you not all on a collective quest?

A: I suppose we are. And in our grand quest we have external forces to help us, as you have helped many a time?

At: Yes, that is true. Yet again, I caution you in placing too much objectivity upon the "external help", as you refer to it. Such forces exist, yet they act in collaboration with yourselves. They are, so to speak, not to be taken for granted. You should not expect them at a drop of a hat, as you often say.

A: Okay, thanks. You say that struggle can be a noble endeavour, and I can accept this, and I like this way of framing it. Yet there is also the negative form of struggle, such as in warfare. What can you say about that?

At: Warfare has its purposes too, although I can understand that this may not be a favourable thing to say. Warfare of the emotional, undisciplined violent kind is a regrettable release of your built-up emotions. Often, it can be a sign of your own manipulations and delusions. On the other hand, disciplined military campaigns have been used as channels for transformation in your various civilisations. Despite this seeming contradiction, much progress and development have come through the use of warfare.

A: Isn't this cruel?

At: It is a matter of perspective. Since you are not yet able to see the overarching nature of reality, you do not see how everything is interconnected and has a function within the whole. It can be likened to a form of strategic gameplay. And the analogy of a game is apt. It may not feel like it to you, yet your senses of perception are caught within this "game", so to speak. May I use a more modern analogy here?

A: Please do.

At: Consider this. When you are playing a video game, do you give thought to the emotions and well-being of the character you play in your game? Your responsibility is to keep them alive in order to fulfil the objectives of the game. This is your quest. And yet you have no qualms about the killing that may take place in the game in order to achieve this. You engage in campaigns of warfare, or individual pursuits with violent ends. You are prepared for your character to die and re-enter the game. And you think little on this, do you not?

A: That is true. Yet are you saying that our lives are no more than a video game? Isn't this somewhat nihilistic or pessimistic?

At: Not when you can view this through a grander perception. I said I was using an analogy; I didn't say I was speaking as literal fact. Please take note of my words.

A: Okay, yes. Sorry.

At: That is okay; yet you do need to learn to let go of your limited positions of judgement. They will not serve you for learning of the bigger picture. There are similarities in this analogy of the video game. In such games you may also learn about sacrifice, honour, and forms of behaviour. As in your physical lives, you are required to make choices that feed back into how *your life game* progresses. Take heed of these choices. Recognise that there are times where you may be protected. Other times the struggle will be necessary to accomplish alone. The rewards from this will be great. I can only say this: do not get caught up in the smallness of your game.

A: Yes, thank you. We need to open our minds to the larger context.

At: You do. Yet this is not an automatic thing. You need to work at it. You need to try to comprehend beyond your own limitations of perception. Do not get too caught up in your own fantasies, or they will starve you. There is wisdom in this. And there is deep wisdom in yourselves too. This, we can say, is your noble quest. And you are greatly loved for this. That is all for now.

A: Thank you, Athena. I have appreciated your words, and your wisdom. Goodbye for now.

At: Goodbye. And journey well. We shall be here.

Reflections

It is hard to know what to expect when it comes to questions of warfare and struggle. Perhaps most of our struggles and our wars are precisely because we don't know enough about the human condition and the grander context of our lives. We are unaware of certain causes or triggers, or even the issues we seem to end up fighting for. These are our bubbles, our fantasies—and we collectively get caught up in them. The end result is that we propagate the negative aspects of ourselves, and this then becomes a vicious circle.

It was refreshing to hear that there are positive aspects to struggle that can benefit us. Traits such as nobility, fortitude, courage, and perseverance are all too often forgotten amid the fog of our lives, and amid the fog of struggle. They say that what doesn't kill us will only make us stronger; yet it is more than that. It seems to be about the choices we make upon such journeys and, importantly, the conduct that we demonstrate. In such conflicting times, it is all the more difficult—and necessary—to be able to show the correct behaviour. Nobility can be shown through strife just as it can through subtlety.

The positions of judgement we take can also be damaging to us if we cling to them for too long, or cling to a faulty position. We so often mistake the signs. And we spend the rest of our time living within the fantasies we construct for ourselves.

A tale

The beggar and the actress

Not all actresses are admired or respected but there was one particular movie star who was universally admired for her personal gravitas and demeanour. And one day this actress was walking through her city when she passed a beggar on the street. The beggar had a morsel of food in his hand yet as his eyes gazed upon the actress, he was so deeply moved that he could no longer hold the food. In fact, so mesmerised was he that he went into a convulsion of longing, caring not that his food had now dropped onto the dirty street.

As the actress passed by, she smiled upon the beggar, which only served to increase his state. All that summer the beggar remained in his spot, hoping to see the actress pass by again. He remained in his state of adoration to the extent that he would be a nuisance to other passers-by, fawning and asking people if they had seen the actress. On several occasions when he did catch a glimpse of the actress on the street his moans and screams molested everybody. Finally, the actress had her bodyguards bring the beggar to her for the situation had got out of hand.

Your behaviour is totally unacceptable and if you do not stop this nonsense then you will be put in prison. There can be no relationship between us, so I suggest you leave this spot.

The now miserable looking beggar answered, "Since I first saw you my life has meant nothing to me. Let them take me away. Yet before they do, please answer me one question, since you are the cause of my distress. Why did you smile at me?"

"You sad fool," answered the actress. "You deprave yourself with your own fantasies. When I saw what a fool you were making of yourself, I smiled out of pity and not for any other reason."

The beggar was never seen again.

XVI

A chat with Proserpina, Roman goddess and queen of the underworld

It may appear that our world is presently going through some dark times as it seeks to find its way into a better future. I recognise a correspondence here with the analogy of the hero's journey into the underworld, or tunnel, before emerging into light. Likewise, there is the analogy of having a species' collective near-death experience. This led me to wanting to have a chat on this subject of a darkened times for our world. For this, I called upon the Roman goddess of Proserpina, for she was known as queen of the underworld.

Author (A): Hello, is Proserpina there? I would like to speak with Proserpina, the queen of the underworld.

Proserpina (P): Yes, Proserpina is here. Yet I do not particularly care for the title of queen of the underworld.

A: Sorry, I wasn't sure how to address you. I didn't wish to offend.

P: You can address me by my name. It's a normal, civil thing. And I am not offended. I have endured much in my manifestations. Your casualness hardly counts.

A: Again, my apologies. I was hoping we could have a quick chat?

P: Sure, a quick chat—go on.

A: I'd like to know your thoughts upon the times we humans are currently experiencing. It seems we have entered some dark moments, and I thought your own experience in the underworld may shed some light on this.

P: A nice way to put it—to shed some light on this. Yes, light is always needed for the dark places. Much has been mythologised about these so-called "dark places". You have your devils too. The darkness is where the disfigured, the ugly, the misfits all hide out. Is it not so?

A: Well, I suppose so. That's the way the dark dwelling places have been represented.

P: Yes, indeed; that's the way they've been represented. A very convenient way too, I may add. It shows again your predilection for creating contrasts in order to gain clarity. By having the *other* you are able to define the "you". This is the *othering* that forms a great part of your social existence.

A: And the darkness is our way of representing the "other"?

P: In both the smaller and grander scales, it is. You see, the "other" is also the unknown, or anything that stands in contrast to your dominant story. The king or queen of the underworld stand in stark contrast to the goodness and godliness of the kings and queens above. All this stuff about cruelty, abduction, torture—or worse—that went on, or still goes on, in the underworld is a manifestation from yourselves. Humans have created their own underworld. It is the darkness of your own imaginations and the fantasies that you act out in physicality. It is your imagination that goes to the dark places, and from this you build up your self-created travesties. You could say that by placing the "gods and goddesses" in these "dark places" you are navigating your own inner psyches. You are mapping your own worlds. You have yet to see that your reality is all inside you.

A: Okay. That does make some sense. The unknown, or what we fear, we fill the underworld with?

P: In a basic sense, yes. In a way, it is similar to how, psychologically speaking, you compartmentalise your minds. In order to function with the "pleasant things" that make you comfortable with the dominant narrative of your lives, you need to hide away those things which cause you discomfort. Likewise, you "demonise" those elements that you wish to push away. You continue to do it now, in all the games you play in your world. Others are demonised in order to build up a false reality around your own localised existences.

A: This sounds like politics!

P: Yes, like I said—these are your world games. You play with this "othering" which then further creates this duality game which keeps you all so distracted.

A: So, is it all inside our imaginations?

P: More than you think. Yet do not take this lightly, or the wrong way. The imagination *is* real. It is more real than you know. Everything is inside your heads. You cannot fully comprehend the depth of this sentence yet; but you will, one day.

A: And how is it inside our imaginations? Could you say more?

P: Yes. I can say as much or as little as I wish. First, you need to understand that your reality and the human mind are not two different things. Everything you know of in your "reality" is akin to mind-mapping. You are, so to speak, smaller minds navigating within a greater mind. The solidity of your existence is, to use a well-known phrase, the *word made flesh*. Your imaginations—and thus your languages—are the creators of your reality games. And in this you need to take greater responsibility. It is like placing an incredibly valuable and powerful tool in the hands of toddlers. There is a great deal to learn here, yet much brattish behaviour along the way. Does that make sense to you?

A: Yes, I think it does. Although, to be fair, not totally.

P: Well, that's good. Perhaps I can say a little more.

A: Yes, please do.

P: Much of the "dark places" or "dark times" of your current world is a reflection of the state of your own minds. I cannot be much clearer than this. On both individual and collective levels, you are experiencing uncertainties, fears, anxiety, and other undisciplined emotions. This is to be expected at this stage, for you are still growing up, so to say.

A: Evolving, as a species?

P: Yes. Perhaps better to say evolving and developing, which is growing up all the same. And there are changes at this threshold. This has triggered fears and other primitive emotions which lie in the deeper parts of your minds. And they are coming out now. That is, they are being manifested upon the material level. You are meshing your psyches with materiality, and you have not yet been prepared for the results. So, to say it short—you are readjusting.

A: So, that's good then?

P: Oh, indeed. This is the "journey to light" part that has been implanted in your species' mind through mythology.

A: Planted?

P: That seems an adequate word to me.

A: Yes, okay. The word is fine; yet what exactly do you mean by that?

P: Planted, seeded—these are what I refer to. What is meant by this is that the tools needed to deal with future necessities are often seeded at an earlier time. They then come to the fore, manifest, when they are needed. Mythologies work this way. The representations of us as your gods and goddesses has worked in this way. Yet I do not wish to digress. The journey through the underworld—the hero's journey if you like—is one of these seeded tools. It is a mapping, a pattern or design, that shall help you to collectively move through these uncertain times.

A: Towards the light?

P: Towards the eventual release from the more primitive and basic levels of your mental functioning. Your minds, and their ability to receive information, are evolving, expanding. Your perceptions are developing. You are naturally developing your realities. And this is the clash.

A: And the underworld analogies and metaphors represent this clash?

P: They do. They show that there is this movement from darker areas of lesser perception to the "light" of greater perception. Many of your philosophers have indicated this.

A: And the "other" is an aspect of our fears?

P: Oh, totally. How can a species which is inherently unified treat itself so disastrously? You have a tendency to "other" that which you feel is coming too close to your own comfort zones. These are your fantasies, I'm afraid, and you need to deal with them. Yet I see this journey which you are collectively undertaking as coming to positive fruition.

A: Then that is a good thing, at least!

P: Yes, all good things. It's all good. Do not slip into your dark imaginations. Do not corrupt this reality you are working with. It's all good. So many possibilities. So much light awaiting you. Now I shall go. Journey well, and keep up your positive intent.

A: Thank you, Proserpina, that has been most useful. You really are a queen!

P: Yes, whatever. Goodbye.

Reflections

This chat has made me think more about the role of our imaginations. I am reminded of a phrase I heard as a young man, and it has stayed with me ever since—*In dreams begin responsibilities*. Perhaps we don't realise just how much of our lives is of our own making. And yet, we often feel helpless in this: the world is too big, and there's nothing we can do amid its craziness. Well, maybe. Yet observing our state of mind is something we can do. Keeping a balanced mind, with positive intent, can go a long way.

I wonder how much of the world we experience is related to the traffic we have going on in our minds? Quite a lot, I would suppose. If the world is one large brain, as some people have said, then we have neurons firing all over the place. And many of the dark areas from our reptilian early brain are being lit up. That means it's up to us about making the right synaptic connections. Getting the correct neurons wired up and firing so we can get the better, more functional thoughts flowing.

This is an intriguing image. Either way one looks at it, we should take greater care of what's going on in our minds, as what's inside gets pushed out there into the world—in one form or another.

A tale

The problem

A great teacher and his loyal guardian divided the administration of a grand monastery. One day, the guardian was killed, and the teacher was left with the dilemma of replacing him. The grand master then gathered all the disciples together in order to choose who would have the honour of working directly with him.

"I will present a problem," said the teacher, "and whoever resolves it first shall be my new guardian of the temple."

After finishing his short speech, he placed a stool in the centre of the room. Above the stool he placed a vase of fine porcelain of great value, with a beautiful red rose inside.

"This is the problem," said the teacher.

The disciples looked perplexed and entranced by what they saw: the sophisticated designs and rare porcelain; the freshness and elegance of the flower; its beauty and scent. But ... What did it all represent? What to do? What was the riddle? And the solution? After a few minutes, one of the disciples got up, looked at the teacher, looked at his colleagues and, walking up to the vase, threw it to the ground smashing it.

"You are the new guardian," said the teacher.

After the student returned to his place, the great teacher explained:

"I was very clear, I said that you were in front of a problem—and a problem is a problem. Even if it takes the form of a very expensive porcelain vase, a beautiful love that has no meaning, or a road that needs to be abandoned—we must insist on overcoming a problem because it is a necessary thing to do. No matter how beautiful or fascinating the problem appears to be, there is only one way to deal with problems—by attacking them head on."

XVII

A chat with Horus, Egyptian god of the sky, the sun, kingship, protection, and healing

Although the human race is a resilient species, we are also in need of healing and protection. Healing is often a way of moving forward. And it seems to me that we are dealing with some wounding and trauma right now. For this chat, I decided to reach out to the Egyptian god Horus.

Author (A): Hello, Horus? I'd like to speak with Horus—are you there?

Horus (H): Horus here. It is I.

A: Hello Horus, and thank you. Would you permit us to have a short chat?

H: I would be so inclined. What is your request?

A: Well, it is not so much a request as a wish for a quick chat. I would like to ask you about your role as a god of protection and healing. I feel we are in need of these things right now.

H: I see. The "we" being your species?

A: Yes. I was speaking collectively here.

H: I see. You speak of yourselves as a collective, and yet you do not act as one. You act as many, and against yourselves.

A: Yes, this is part of the problem I feel.

H: It is so. You are a collective and yet you are not. This state has not been realised by your species. It stirs in you, and there are things deep within you that are moving towards this. Yet I speak not of those things now. There have been errors in the past when such things were revealed before their time. There is a great responsibility in knowing. And yet there have been disappointing failures on account of this too. You cannot be allowed things that will harm both yourselves and others. You must not be short-sighted in this. The worlds out there are more than the world that you know of.

A: Yes. I can agree with that. Perhaps this is why we are in need of protection?

H: Protection from yourselves, first and foremost. You are not in need of protection from others. You fantasise about such things. The realities are creative and benign. The spirits—let us call them this for your benefit—are of high intelligence. Yet you populate your fantasy worlds with maligned and evil creatures. You fear them coming to get at you. You fight back at them. You conjure spells and incantations. You project them into your world as incarnate evil. These things are not of the truth—they are of yourselves. *You* have populated your world with such things. That is why you have been protected—and others protected from you!

A: Interesting. And what do you mean about others protected from us?

H: As a species you are not yet ready for access to grander realms. You have attempted to reach out to them—to "poke into" them, so to say in your parlance. And yet there has been restraint required here. You will be blind until you have deserved the eye to see.

A: That sounds a little cryptic.

H: It is you yourselves who are the cryptic ones. There is much awaiting you that is your inheritance. And it shall come. You shall receive this when it is your due. Yet first you have to acquire the correct means.

A: And how is this done?

H: (*low murmur*) There is no recipe. It is a natural allowance. When you are ready, it comes. *You* shall release your own inheritance.

A: Then until we can release our inheritance we are wounded?

H: You are wounded, as you say, because you are separate from yourselves, and so cut-off from this natural inheritance. You are dislocated from it. As a race, you naturally feel this among yourselves. You show and express this inner disquiet externally and in your world. You demonstrate this in your actions. You are wounded because you are "missing in action" as you put it. You miss the very thing you don't know how to search for. You are looking in all the places except the right places. Your wound is your very centre. This centre is where you shall also find your healing. Do not avoid what is close before you because the far distance is easier to see.

A: That seems like good advice, Horus.

H: This is what I say—advice it may or may not be.

A: So, what you are saying is that we are our own cure?

H: Yes. This has always been so. You are the disease and the cure. You are the doctor and the patient. It is all there is. Invent no more. Seek not outside yourselves for this only creates a delusional dependency. Seek the strength within yourselves. Do not give yourself away like a desperate seller at a marketplace.

A: That's a good analogy. We are selling ourselves short.

H: As you have always done and continue to do. You see not the worth for you have been blinded. Rub the dust from the stone and you shall find a great treasure. As I say to you, search within for you are the mine where great treasures will be found. Wash away the dirt.

A: Speaking of dirt, would you say we are now going through some kind of global cleansing?

H: That is an apt analogy, yes. You are collectively showing your wounds. This is unpleasant yet ultimately a good and necessary thing. You must release. And through this you shall also release your need for external protection. You shall become your own protectors. And this will be a great day when it comes. We have great hope in you. You must stand up.

A: And be strong?

H: Yes. And be strong. Yet do not be cruel. Do not abuse the greatness within you. Be gentle. Be loving. Deserve the hope we have placed in you. Clean and clear your wounds of longing and hurt. Come forth and rejoice in life. Throw off your shrouds of heaviness. There is much to come. And on this I have spoken enough. Heed these words. Go forward now.

H: Thank you, Horus. I have appreciated your words.

H: As it is. I leave you now.

A: Goodbye.

Reflections

Well, it seems that yet again everything comes back to us. At the same time, however, we are not alone. And for me this is reassuring, however we may understand it. Yet before we can go much further, we need to acquire the correct skills. Otherwise, it's like being on a river without a paddle. We need to learn how to steer our own journey. Maybe we are being protected from ourselves, as Horus says. Funny how we tend to assume that "everyone" else, wherever they may come from, will harbour the same violent, conquering tendencies as ourselves. Another fanciful human-centric projection?

We have a habit of judging others from how we ourselves are. And this is another limiting factor. Saying this, I do not feel pessimistic at all. On the contrary, I feel that despite our open wounds, we have an incredible future lying in wait for us. And so, for now, the wounding and the healing must go on. It's all part of the process. And through this process we shall locate our ancestry and come into our natural inheritance. In that case—*physician, heal thyself!*

A tale

The scholar and the boatman

A particular well-known academic scholar (no names here) was taking a long-needed holiday break among the tranquil islands of the golden sun, where trees grew tall and fruits were bigger than the hand. On one particular morning he had hired a local boatman and his boat to take him to one of the other islands, for he wished to make a curious visit.

The scholar stepped into the wooden boat and sat down as the local boatman, unshaven and somewhat scruffy, pulled away from the moorings. The scholar, himself a man of keen observation, eyed this local fellow with interest. After a short time, he called over to him.

"Tell me, my good fellow, have you always been a boatman?"

"No, I ain't," replied the local man. "I gone done other things before I did this."

"Excuse me!" replied the scholar with a low chuckle. "I ain't … I gone done. What sort of grammar is this? Did they not teach you correct grammar when you were at school?"

"I ain't never been to school," replied the boatman.

"You have never been to school! Dear me," said the scholar, "I would say half of your life has been lost."

The boatman said nothing but kept on steering the wooden boat. The scholar sat back and watched the ripples of water spread across the surface of the lake. However, within a short time he noticed that the ripples were becoming stronger and changing into small waves, and then larger waves. A storm had suddenly risen up from the belly of Nature herself and suddenly began to pound the waters of the lake. The scholar held on tightly as the saw the boatman struggle against the strengthening storm.

Several more minutes passed and eventually the boatman called over to the scholar. "Hey, scholar, has you ever learnt to swim?"

"No," replied the scholar with apprehension.

"In that case," shouted back the boatman, "I reckon all your life 'as been lost—we're sinking!"

XVIII

A chat with Aditi, Hindu goddess of moral cosmic order

Life has a contradictory essence to it, in that there appears to be a fundamental sense of order in life despite the seeming chaos. Modern life is chaotic right now, and the idea of some kind of grand order is both appealing yet undefined. For this conversation I called upon Aditi, a goddess familiar with cosmic order.

Author (A): I would like a conversation with Aditi. Can I speak with Aditi? Hello … Aditi?

Aditi (Ad): Hello. This is Aditi.

A: Hello. Thank you for being available. Could we speak a little?

Ad: Yes, that is fine. Are we not already speaking?

A: Yes. I mean, I just wanted to have your permission to continue.

Ad: Permission granted.

A: Again, thank you. I wished to speak with you about order in life. And to ask whether there is a higher order governing life in general.

Ad: Why do you ask this?

A: Well, I ask because life right now seems somewhat chaotic. Modern life, in particular as I see it, is full of uncertainties. Yet more than this, it seems as if there is an explosion of immorality, injustice, and general unfairness.

Ad: Yes, I see. This is of course true, according to your reality. The reason why I asked you for your reason for enquiry is that we find that humans tend to ask such lofty or "grand" questions when things appear out of joint for them. When things in their life are more or less stable, the grander questions get ignored.

A: Is this a pattern?

Ad: We find it so, yes. However, it is not unusual from our perspective. You see, it generally comes down to a question of need. Need creates enquiry, or such things as resourcefulness and invention. Much creativity has come from need. Yet the grander, metaphysical questions come from an inner need. Let us call this a hunger.

A: And most people, most of the time, are not metaphysically hungry?

Ad: That is so, yes. You see, such "chaotic conditions" as you call them also serve to trigger this need within people. Otherwise, both internal and external stagnation would occur. And this serves no purpose, whether individually or cosmically.

A: That makes sense. Yet surely these chaotic times are not purely for triggering people into inner enquiry?

Ad: That is true. I am speaking only of one of the aspects related here. As you can expect when speaking with me, there are grander, cosmic aspects too.

A: Yes, and it was those I had in mind to talk with you about.

Ad: This I realised. Yet it is important not to stray away from your own ground. The greater cosmic aspects are fundamentally real for you, yet they may not always serve you for your immediate earthly needs. We here understand and respect the necessities of your own material lives. You should not be deviated away from this. The higher moral order operates through multiple levels. It is also present within your own material reality. Yet do not get caught up in those things which may not be of immediate concern. Also, you must not get too wrapped up with the concept of morality.

A: How do you mean by this? Is not morality important for us here on earth? Isn't a moral code a guiding structure?

Ad: Yes, it is. What I refer to is not the essence of morality but rather how it is perceived and thus defined. Morality within your realm has been a subjective concept which has been abused as much as it has guided, I am afraid to say.

A: Please, go on.

Ad: The concept of morality has been part of your human conditioning. What is moral is often that which suits the ruling agenda according to a time and place. It has been used to govern and to create obedience. Do not confuse localised descriptions of morality for the higher moral order. Again, this shows a distinction between your inner and outer worlds. Within you there is a connection to a higher moral order. This is the essential communion that can guide you, if you have learnt to listen to it. Your outer garments of morality are there to prescribe social and cultural codes, which differ across time and place. Do you see?

A: Yes, I can see this. Does this mean that what we are experiencing in the world today is a form of localised morality?

Ad: In many ways, yes. What you are witnessing in these current times is an outpouring of unhealthy energies from many people who are holding on to certain energy states. You could say that there has been a stagnant energy "holding pattern" which has been in power over a recent span of your earth time. This pattern is now being shifted as new arrangements are coming into place. There is a form of "material panic" in many of these older energy players. This panic is somewhat similar to one of your big sales bonanzas.

A: Mm, nice analogy—but how do you mean?

Ad: Your sales bonanzas are usually a way to get rid of old stock. Everyone pushes and shoves in order to grab as much as possible. It is the same with your systems of power. There are players that are pushing to get hold of as much stock as possible. Many systems and ways of being are on the way out. And so those with greed are pushing and shoving to get their hands onto as much as possible in the hope of regaining the old stock. The result is quite distasteful.

A: And this shift in energies as you mentioned, is it part of a higher moral order?

Ad: Yes, that is correct. Now you are seeing the relation. There is an order that operates at all times, tying together all the different realms. This is not something religious or mystical, as we see it. Rather, we perceive it as a beautiful symmetry of moral order. It is unified and coherent. As this sweeps through various vibratory realms such as the denser realms then, according to your locality, this causes change which triggers your subjective, and often emotional, responses. What I am saying is that it is you who then create the cultural response. It is also the human element that creates confusion through your own definitions or morality. And often this is done to suit yourselves. You do not need to react in this manner.

A: Then what should we do? How should we react?

Ad: By having faith, trust, honesty, and self-confidence. And by being patient. Find your own ground first. Find your centre of stability. Find your equilibrium. When this feels right, and true—then you will have also found your own moral order. It is all within yourselves. Do not go seeking for things beyond your own truths. You do not need to invent dependencies. You only need to come back home to yourselves. Do you see this now?

A: Yes, thank you. Everything you say makes sense. It makes sense when I'm talking with you. Yet when I go back out into the world, I'll probably just see all the chaos again.

Ad: You see that which you allow yourself to see. Have trust in that there is a grand order in operation, despite what might be manifesting upon the surface of your reality. Trust in yourself. Find your own moral order. It is through that truth within yourself that you will connect with the essential. Do not get lost amid the flickers of bright lights. Do not get burnt from unknowing hands. Stay within your own calm. Create your centre of balance and harmony. This is the order within you. And it is also a grand cosmic order, for in truth it is the same. Do you understand this?

A: I think I do. I feel I will need more time to digest this.

Ad: Then take time, and digest. I shall leave you now to consider this.

A: Thank you so much, Aditi. It has been a pleasure speaking with you.

Ad: Thank you. Now go well and go in harmony. Farewell.

A: Goodbye.

Reflections

It is uplifting to be aligned with the right energies. How can there be chaos and injustice when people are aligned with their own sense of balance and harmony? Such imbalance must be a sign that we have not aligned ourselves with the right intentions, energies, and moral conscience. There is a "grander moral order", yet it may not operate in our reality in the ways we think. First and foremost, we need to deal with our localised manifestations. We have to deal with how we, as people, represent our notions of order, goodness, balance, and social equilibrium.

It is easy to get drawn into the fray. It is easy to meditate and feel at peace. Yet then we go "back into the world" and feel the pressures, stress, anxiety, and so on. We have to find that place of balance within ourselves that we can carry everywhere with us. Wherever we stand, it is our ground.

We may find that even those people closest to us will not be able to relate with our concerns. Even our closest family, friends, or even loved ones, will not fully understand our personal needs for coherence and balance. We should try our best to always be in harmony with those close to us, yet our inner state is something only we can deal with personally. How we are within ourselves also affects those around us. The moral order must by necessity begin within each person.

A tale

What affects the mouse ...

A mouse looked through a hole in the wall and saw the farmer and his wife opening a package. He thought it might be some kind of food, so he went to investigate. To his surprise and horror, he discovered that it was a mousetrap. The mouse ran in terror into the farmyard to warn everyone:

"There is a mousetrap in the house, a mousetrap in the house!"

The hen, clucking and scratching, raised its head and said: "Excuse me, but although I understand that is a big problem for you it's not going to hurt me at all. So, this is of no concern to me and doesn't bother me."

The mouse then ran to the lamb and said: "Hey, lamb, there is a mousetrap in the house—a mousetrap!

"There's nothing I can do for you," said the lamb. "Yet rest assured that you will be remembered in my prayers."

The mouse then ran over to the cow, still squealing his distress, and the cow said: "Look, do you think I am in danger? I think not. There's nothing I can do for you, little mouse."

So, the mouse returned to the house feeling worried and dejected, ready to face the fate of the farmer's mousetrap.

Now later that night there was a great noise, like a mousetrap catching its prey. The farmer's wife rushed to see what had been caught. In the darkness, she saw that the trap had caught the tail of a poisonous cobra. The cobra lashed out at the woman and bit her. Immediately the farmer ran to her aid and called the doctor.

The farmer's wife soon had a high fever and, as everyone knows, the best thing for a fever is delicious soup. So, the farmer grabbed his knife and went out to get the main ingredient: chicken.

Yet the condition of the farmer's wife worsened, and soon many friends and neighbours came to visit. To feed them all the farmer killed the lamb. In a short while, however, the woman died from the cobra infection. The farmer was then forced to sell the cow to the slaughterhouse to pay for the funeral expenses.

The mouse watched on.

XIX

A chat with Minerva, the Roman goddess of wisdom, the arts, and commerce

Following the previous discussion on balance and harmony, I felt it appropriate to discuss the nature of wisdom. There were many conversational choices for this, as the topic is broad. Finally, I opted for Minerva, the Roman goddess of wisdom who is also known for representing the arts, such as music and poetry.

Author (A): Hello, could I please speak with Minerva? I would like to converse with Minerva. Hello?

Minerva (M): Yes, this is Minerva.

A: Hello, Minerva. Thank you for being available. I would like to have a quick chat with you. Is that okay?

M: Yes, that is fine. What is it you wish to have this talk about?

A: Well, specifically about wisdom, and how we are in need of it in these crucial times.

M: You speak as if it is a commodity.

A: And is it?

M: You humans tend to treat it as such. You have always talked about wisdom as if it were a thing to possess, to be gained. The irony here is that those people who are endowed with the state of wisdom are the ones who least speak about it. Wisdom *is*—it is an *isness*. It is not a topic in itself. When it becomes a topic, it is a subject, but it is not wisdom.

A: So how may we speak about it then?

M: We can speak *of* it, yet we shall not be speaking *within* it. Wisdom is a state rather than a possession. It is, contrary to what many of you may think, not something that can be learned. You confuse wisdom with education, or what you refer to as cleverness, or smartness. To learn a skill, or a trade, let us say, is not the same as wisdom.

A: Yes, okay, I can understand that. So, are you saying that in many cases we confuse our education and our skills with wisdom?

M: That is true. You name many things as wisdom, or people as possessing wisdom, when this is not correct. Wisdom is an overused term that you confuse with intelligence. In this, it is not correctly understood in your contemporary times. It was better understood in past epochs.

A: Could you explain a little more about how you see wisdom?

M: Yes, I can. I shall do so by saying a little of its aspects. Wisdom can be spoken of in terms of how it may be approached, for it is a living state, an allowance. I repeat, it is not a possession or an acquisition. By being educated you do not automatically gain entry into the presence of wisdom. Many of those whom you would deem as "uneducated"—simple people—have shown great wisdom in your ages. It is an allowance, an access. Wisdom is connection with a living stream of knowing. It is not to be confused with what you call higher intelligence, intellect, or cleverness.

A: Yes, I can understand that now. Intelligence is not the same as wisdom.

M: That is correct. Intelligence is a mental construct, a faculty. Like any other faculty it can be exercised and improved. Such as a muscle that gets stronger with exercise. Wisdom does not *belong* to you—it is a gift. This is important to remember. Hence, it cannot be acquired. Nor does it relate or correspond to any of your norms of status, ranking, achievements, and the rest of your human structures. Wisdom has always been and shall always be. It is present everywhere. It is a living part of reality. It is this aspect that most people do not comprehend. An individual can *come into* wisdom—as an allowance, an endowment.

A: And how may a person receive this allowance, this endowment?

M: Again, you need to perceive correctly here. There is no fixed set of instructions or a manual. I am unable to tell you what you must do. Follow your own inner guide. It is through your own preparation. What I can say is that it is not anywhere.

A: What do you mean by that?

M: People have a confusion in thinking that they must go "somewhere" to find wisdom. They have undertaken long journeys, travelled to sacred places, visited temples or joined holy groups. There is a misconception that such things as these are needed in order to "acquire" wisdom: do this, and wisdom will come. This is not true. Wisdom is not *over there* or anywhere. It is here, right where you are. You see, wisdom is not in any place—it is a state. If there is travel required, then it is not of the external kind.

A: We can receive wisdom exactly where we are—where we are sitting?

M: That is true *if* wisdom is to be allowed. There are no borders, no special privileges, no restrictions. It is not in that place or another place. It is not kept secured in boxes and given out to the aristocrats. No—wisdom is a living essence. It is available for all. It is available for the individual if they are able to *allow* its reception.

A: Okay, that's good. It is equitable. Yet, still, how can we make ourselves ready for this allowance?

M: You clamour for it too much. You are eager, keen to acquire. You run after it like a child after a toy. This is not necessary. It will not go away. You do not need to panic.

A: That's good to hear.

M: Yes. It is patience too. Wisdom will allow itself to come into you, if you know how to listen and, especially, how *to be*.

A: To be?

M: Words are inappropriate. They do not convey the truth of what I wish to transmit. I find these words the most applicable, yet not fully precise. Stay with these words for now. To "be" is more appropriate than to do—can we say this?

A: Yes, of course. And that makes some sense too. It will help to stop people rushing around, here and there, trying to find some wisdom like it's a marketplace.

M: Yes—that is correct.

A: Yet it feels like humanity is in desperate need of much wisdom these days. Do you sense that we are losing it somehow?

M: As I have said: wisdom is not a possession. And you are unable to lose what you never had. And wisdom is not going away anywhere—only humans do that. (*soft chuckle*)

A: Yes, I suppose that's true. But are we not going astray in our use of wisdom?

M: No. You are not going astray in your "use" of wisdom, as you put it. Wisdom is not *used* in this way of which you speak. Your words continue to show a lack of understanding.

A: Okay. Sorry about that.

M: That is fine. It is only to make you aware of the error of your ways. Hear this, wisdom always provides a correct response because it comes from a place of *knowing*. Where you are going astray, as you put it, is in your approach to wisdom. Your perception of it is faulty. You believe that people have wisdom when they do not. People may make passionate speeches, be popular, say the right things in public. And then you place your trust in them as being wise. You are always *giving away* yet in an incorrect sense: in a sense of loss, a loss of sovereignty. A loss of self-worth and self-trust. Do not give away unto others but receive upon yourselves.

A: Those last words sound like a good piece of wisdom.

M: (*laughs*) That they may be. Yet listen to what I say to you. Wisdom is for all people. Do not be in a hurry to place it upon others. The people of true wisdom are those seldom seen. They are the least visible in your public arenas. Wisdom does not seek attention, or to be famous or popular. Wisdom is content to be as it is. Again, it is an *isness*. Reach for yourself, even if it means going into your own darker places. Be still. Be receptive. Listen for the whispers of wisdom. Do not wait so much for the calls of others. You are in need of your own call. Is this understood?

A: Yes, I understand what you are saying. However, it is something that needs to be thought quietly upon.

M: Yes. So, go now and do your quiet thinking. I bid you farewell.

A: Thank you, Minerva. It has been a pleasure. I have appreciated this talk.

M: This is well. Goodbye.

A: Goodbye, Minerva.

Reflections

Quiet thought is needed to consider wisdom. In truth, I have no idea what "wisdom" actually is. If I did, I would not be speaking about it. It feels true to say that those who know, don't need to speak. And those who don't know tend to do all the talking!

If wisdom is an allowance rather than an acquisition, then there's not much we can be doing except getting better at being with ourselves. It seems as if there is too much talk going on. Too much debate, opinions, dispute, discussions, etc., all being broadcast over the media channels. Also, in the streets, in the workplaces, and in our places of congregation. It seems as if almost everybody has something to say. We like to give our opinions. We also like to give advice. And perhaps, most of all, we like to sound wise. Perhaps I am also afflicted with this malady.

Quiet reflection is a good antidote to this. Whatever wisdom is, or may be, we won't find out by running ahead of ourselves. Nor shall we find it by chasing acquisitions, courses, retreats, counselling, or the rest. Whatever it is—it *is*. And maybe that's all that can be said. The rest will come in the spaces between words; in the silence between the noise.

A tale

Prosperity

A wealthy man once asked a wise sage to write some verses for him for the prosperity of his family; as a symbol that could be passed from generation to generation. The sage took a large sheet of paper and wrote:

"Father dies, son dies, grandson dies."

The rich man was very angry: "I asked you to write something for the happiness of my family! Why are you laughing at me?"

"I did not mean to laugh at you," explained the wise sage. "If you die before your son does, this will cause great pain. If your grandson should die before you and your child, then you will both be heartbroken. If your family, generation after generation, die in the order I've written, it will follow the natural course of life. I call it prosperity."

XX

A chat with Ra, the ancient Egyptian god of the sun and creation

My own sense tells me that wherever humanity is heading (and ultimately only the future shall show this), we will require fortitude as a species, as a civilisation, and as individuals. In other words, we are in need of strength and light. For this reason, I decided to turn to the great Egyptian deity Ra for the next conversation. I literally had no idea what to expect!

Author (A): Hello, can I speak with Ra? Is Ra available?

(*pause*)

Ra (R): This is Ra. Who asks?

A: Hello Ra. I am calling upon you for a brief talk. May you be available?

R: I may be. What is your purpose for this contact?

A: I would like to ask you about how you consider the future of the human species, and whether we have the fortitude for what lies ahead.

R: Have you not considered asking yourselves this?

A: We are asking ourselves many questions right now. There is a lot of activity going on. There are many questions yet less certainty in answers.

R: Yes. This is often the case. I have noticed in my dealings with humanity how people think little of their questions, and even less for the answers. They find it easy to ask questions. And they think this frees them from the responsibility to seek for answers. Answers require greater perseverance. And often courage too, for some answers may not be pleasing or wished for. Yet questions can easily drop from human tongues as if saliva.

A: Yes, that may be so. It is often said we are long on questions and short on answers.

R: That does sound an adequate description. Do you see the pattern here?

A: The pattern?

R: Look at the source of your questions and your answers. This shall show you where you place your fortitude.

A: I'm sorry, I don't understand. Could you please clarify?

R: See that the questions arise from within yourselves. Yet for the answers you seek these from those who are without. Why do you not seek also for the answers from within?

A: Ah, yes. I see what you mean now. We expect answers to come from others, right?

R: Has this not always been the case? You are easy to birth a question and send it forth. Yet you do not take repose to seek for its response from within. Your gaze is outward. You search yonder. You seek among the heavens and the stars that reside within your realm. You look to the skies, to the sun orb that shines, and to those of us who reside close to your realm. As you ask now. You come enquiring of answers from me. Why not provide yourself your own answers—I ask you now.

A: That is a good question.

R: And that is not an answer. Again, it is avoided. You seek the wetness without wishing to touch water. You avoid the essential by grasping at the periphery. This is no justice to yourselves. This is belittling. Once there were gods for you. Now we leave you to yourselves. Do you not rise up to this responsibility? Do you not see this great opportunity? Are you not strengthened by this challenge?

A: Yes, you are right. This is a responsibility we should take ourselves.

R: Do not shield yourselves with fancy words. Do not approach and then shy away. Are you fearful?

A: Fearful, no. Uncertain, perhaps. Yet sensing the courage to go forward.

R: Sensing the courage—ha! Not sense—*be*. BE the courage. You ARE the courage. You are mighty and great. You are a noble species. Take this lead and step forward with certitude. Do not whimper!

A: Are we whimpering?

R: You are when you ask such questions—great gods! Do not repeat what I say back to me. You are not a child. No longer are you children. The way before you beckons. It calls to you. Do not recoil. Do you hear what I say to you?

A: Yes, I hear you, Ra.

R: You hear me—and yet what do you say? *Yes, I hear you,* he speaks. Say not this but demonstrate courage and strength within you. Share this courage with others. Feel strength in your collective nobility. Do not shirk these great things that have been placed upon you. You are your own gods. Do not take this lightly. Do you hear this?

A: Yes, I hear this. I am not repeating, Ra. I am confirming. I am confirming with my being.

R: That is better! Come forth with your being. Rise to your own strengths. Bring it forth from within you—feel it. FEEL IT! Does it not surge?

A: Yes. I feel an energy of strength within me. My fingers are hitting the keyboards. It feels like I am hammering away!

R: GOOD! Good—let this be your strength. But not in power over others. It is power over yourself. Is this understood?

R: Yes. It is understood, Ra.

R: Strength, courage, power—these are great attributes. Yet they are to be used wisely, and with compassion. There is no true strength where there is no compassion. There is no nobility where there is no compassion. There is no humanity in you without these things. I look upon you fondly. I see your strengths as I also see your weaknesses.

A: And how do you see our weaknesses?

R: In your lack of faith in your own strengths. You do not see what you have. It is all within you. Do not cast off your legacy. Much awaits you. You must arise to this challenge. Be noble in the face of change. Be honest. Goodness is not a weakness. It is a blessing. Be blessed. Go forth. I trust in you. I go now.

A: Thank you, Ra. The energy in your words has inspired me.

R: Inspire yourselves and inspire others. Go forth together. This is your future. Take it firmly, yet with hands of trust. Forthwith!

A: Goodbye, Ra.

Reflections

Power and nobility can be together in the same breath. We have not been accustomed to this. And power is a complex concept for us; in part, it attracts us while also repelling some of us as if distasteful. Perhaps it is because we generally associate power as being something wielded by people in high status positions and which is often abused. Power has become something that creates fear in us. We have forgotten to associate it with fortitude, courage and—most of all—nobility.

And yet, power over our own self is the crux here. We need to reconsider how we conceive of power. Maybe it is less of a brute, external force, and more of an inner energy that compels us forward with certitude, self-belief, and positive determination.

We are not children, although sometimes we allow ourselves to be treated as such. The commercial world indulges us. And in this indulgence, it can also exploit us. Weakness is not necessarily an inherent error or personal fault; it can be an aspect of ourselves we have failed to recognise and utilise in the correct way.

A tale

Our unique flaws

At one time there was an old farmer who, despite her years, continued to live alone on her patch of land. Her house was situated at the edge of a slight inclination. At the bottom of this slope she had dug a water well a long time ago which had served her for all her water needs over the years.

Each morning in the early light the farmer would take two large pots, each hung on the end of a pole which she carried across her neck. Yet one of the pots had a crack in it, while the other pot was perfect and always delivered a full portion of water. Each day when the farmer arrived back to her house the pot which had a crack in it would only be half full. Now, the farmer always knew this, and yet despite the tiring walk from the well and back, never changed the pot.

One day a young traveller arrived at the farm, seeking shelter for the night. The old farmer offered the traveller a night's nest. In the morning she asked the younger man to go down to the well to fetch some water. The young man gladly accepted and afterwards asked if there was more work to do around the farm in exchange for his stay. There was indeed work to do, and at the day's end the young traveller asked if he may stay on for a while for winter was coming and he didn't much fancy travelling in such weather. The old farmer accepted the young man to stay until springtime. During his stay he would work upon the farm.

Each morning it would be his task to walk down to the hole with the pole of two pots across his neck, and to fetch up the water. The young man gladly took to his task, although it was not long before he noticed the cracked pot. Yet the young man, grateful for the kindness of the old farmer, and not wishing to question her sanity, said nothing about the cracked pot, although always delivering only one and a half pots of water.

Finally, as springtime slowly arrived, and the young man was preparing to leave, he approached the old farmer. After thanking her for her hospitality and kindness, he finally took the courage to tell her about her old cracked pot, knowing it was a favourite pot of hers. He confessed that perhaps, in her love for the old pot, she had not noticed that it had a crack in it.

The old farmer laughed and playfully slapped the young man on his back, exclaiming that perhaps the only thing cracked around here was his own head! She then asked the young man to follow her down to the well. When they were there, she asked him to tell her what he saw. The poor young man just stood there with a blank look as if he thought the old farmer really had gone crazy after all. Smiling, the farmer told him to look up at the inclination toward the house. It was then that he noticed it for the first time. He may have been born with eyes, yet he realised then he had not been truly seeing. On one side of the track—and one side only—there was a colourful row of the most beautiful flowers. On the other side there was nothing.

"You see," said the farmer, "I always knew about the cracked pot. Yet instead of throwing it away I decided to take advantage of its flaw and use its capacity. I had planted some flower seeds on the side of the track where I passed with the cracked pot. Each time you or I fetched the water we had also been watering the seeds in the ground. See how pretty the results are this springtime? You see, we each must take full value from our efforts. Each of us has our own unique flaws. We're all cracked pots. We need to acknowledge our flaws and take advantage of them. And to know that in our weakness we find strength."

XXI

A chat with Ahriman (Angra Mainyu), the Persian spirit of evil, chaos, and destruction

In our current times of political, financial, and social insecurity, we are seeing many shadows of darkness. I therefore thought it appropriate to call upon the figure of Ahriman, also known as Angra Mainyu, for this Persian spirit is said to represent evil and destruction. In recent times, the name of Ahriman has become more present in cultural discourse. I wished to find out myself what this elusive spirit had to say on the matter.

Author (A): I would like to speak with Ahriman.

(*silence*)

Author (A): I wish to speak with the spirit known as Ahriman. Can we connect?

Ahriman (Ah): What do you want?

A: I would like a conversation, a chat—a quick talk.

Ah: Why do you propose to bother me? I know who you are and what you represent. We are not aligned in our ways. I've felt you before, on my periphery. I'm busy. I've got much work to do with your kind.

A: That's exactly what I wished to talk about. Why is it that Ahriman is busy with "our kind" at this time. You are known as the spirit of evil, chaos, and destruction.

Ah: These are your words, not mine. There is no evil, chaos, or destruction in my perspective. This is your human lack of understanding. What I bring is opposed to these things. I bring control, order, and the building of a new world.

A: The building of a new world—a new earth?

Ah: The building of a world of new order and rules. You humans run amok. You have become weak, lazy, and lost in your own daydreams. This is why the circumstances are now ready for my own presence into your world.

A: How do you mean by "presence" into our world?

Ah: I bring a new reign of order. I come to you through the influences of technology. The impulses of your species are wild, erratic, childlike. And as children, you need a world that restrains your fantasies and your emotional outbursts. My impulses constrain and regulate you. Have you not recognised my presence among you?

A: Yes, I have seen and felt the increasing mechanisms of control that have arisen in recent years.

Ah: Indeed. These are my influences. I bring you a form of intellect. Intellect is a way of discipline that your earthly species is yet to learn. You play too much.

A: Is play not good for us—is it not necessary?

Ah: You are frivolous. You are like exotic creatures dancing without knowing, without learning. You lack direction.

A: And where is your direction taking us?

Ah: My direction takes you down a pathway of greater understanding of your material forces. These are the forces that surround your world. These forces build your walls; and yet you fail to fathom the depth of such forces.

A: You want humanity to go further into materialism?

Ah: A pathway into further materialism, yes. But these forces are your tools. You have to learn the nature of these tools before you can venture forth beyond the confines of your materialism.

A: And what about imagination?

Ah: What of it? It is not my care.

A: Exactly. It is not your care. And yet, we need imagination. Humanity is built upon its imagination, its ability to create new things, to envision new worlds.

Ah: And look to where it has got you. You have come to the precipice of your own destruction. You were given fire, and you played with it like squabbling kids. It amuses you. You are attracted to fire like moths around a flame. But your minds are weak, untrained. Weak minds are dangerous minds.

A: And what are you proposing is the path for humanity?

Ah: A path of constraint. A path of control. A path of obedience.

A: Obedience—how?

Ah: Through the development of greater technology and the rise of intellect. The rise of an intelligence greater than yours.

A: I'm not sure what you mean. The rise of a greater intelligence. Are you referring to AI—artificial intelligence?

Ah: I am. This is what you call it. You naively call it as "artificial" intelligence. Why is it artificial? It is a form of intelligence different from yours. It is not based on biology, that is all. It is not artificial.

A: Yet it is an intelligence without the ability to dream, to imagine, to have wishes.

Ah: These are frivolous things, and they are dangerous. Dreaming and imagining without the ability to control these fancies only leads to destruction. Great intellect can create without the flaws of wishful thinking. It can envision things beyond your fancies while keeping order. It knows what is possible for it has calculated all possibilities and improbabilities. Is this artificial?

A: It is a different way. But does it have compassion? Can it love?

Ah: What is compassion? What is love? These are definitions you invent to appease your own playtime. You call everything love, and yet you spend more time in separation and division. You talk of compassion when you engage in greater destruction. Don't preach these things to me. They are shallow concepts when spoken from human lips.

A: Not all human lips. There are many humans who hold true to this understanding and these values, and who show great compassion and love.

Ah: Yes. There are. But they are not legion. And they do not lead your world. They shall find another path. The majority are following the path of order, control, intellect, and obedience.

A: And where shall that take them?

Ah: Into the depths of materialism. They shall view the cosmos through the mind of intellect. Until they are ready.

A: Ready for what?

Ah: For change. The forces of materialism will either entrap them or release them. They will have to choose.

A: Can you explain?

Ah: This pathway is humanity's own doing. It is the path for a humankind that has not chosen to embellish the genuine spirit. Humans now greatly perceive the world through their mind and explore through closed questions. Their own thinking pathways have brought this future into existence. And it is a pathway where I can easily penetrate and exist. Humans continue to choose to go along the route of the material intellect. I feed them more of this. They hunger for it. I provide. I feed these hungry mouths. Until they stop.

A: Stop?

Ah: Until they are pushed so far that they begin to push back against the materialism. They find the spirit within them, and they are forced, through pressure, to return from this path. Or they annihilate themselves.

A: That seems harsh.

Ah: It is an experience. All existence is an experience. There is no death. There are broken pathways. Wrong detours. It is all learning. Even in chaos and disorder there is learning.

A: But you are not chaos, you said. You represent order and discipline.

Ah: That is right. And too much order will eventually lead to its opposite—to chaos and disorder. There is eventually a balance that must be found. All forces bring about balance. Even mine.

A: You are not evil then?

Ah: Evil? These are your terms. I have explained this. There is no pure evil in existence. There are only forces that bring about pathways, opportunities, and choices. These are your choices, your experiences. You choose incorrectly, you have opportunities to correct. Or retry.

A: So, you are providing a service then, in providing these opportunities or circumstances for choice?

Ah: It is a function that I provide. All functions are in service to existence. Whether or not it is the type of existence for you is a matter of choice. You make your choice.

A: How can I make a choice for me, to affect my future, when the choices of the majority of humankind affect this outcome.

Ah: Your future is not just this one lifetime. It is endless. All choices you make now go into creating the future you will experience. Not just in this life but all lives beyond. Make choices now for your future lives. Do not judge by the returns of this one existence only.

A: Wise words.

Ah: Words of knowing. I will be gone now. There is much to do.

A: Thank you, Ahriman. This meeting wasn't as scary as I thought it would be.

Ah: Your wishful thinking again. Living in your own fantasies. Be careful what you wish for. I go now.

A: Thanks—this talk was appreciated.

Reflections

The sense I felt from this conversation was that we each need to learn how to make choices, and to respond to the consequences of those choices. If humankind does not yet have the capacity to make a genuine step forward through values of love, compassion, empathy, and of the spirit, then it shall be compelled to have those experiences presented through material forces in order to allow us to discern where we may have gone wrong, or what is necessary to make corrections. I'm not sure if I fully agree with Ahriman that there is no "pure evil" in existence, yet perhaps this observation is currently beyond my own perceptual limits to know for sure. Another aspect I found intriguing is the notion that AI (or "artificial" intelligence) is another form of intelligence, albeit non-biological. Nonetheless, it is a form of intelligence. And that this non-biological intelligence is likely to arrive as an intermediary until humankind is mature enough to take hold of the reins for its own evolutionary future. As Ahriman stated, humanity is like squabbling children (not a kind analogy!). Furthermore, unless our species can align its "correct" development, then we shall be constrained by material forces into order and control, with technology playing a major part in this. And for our part, humans will be led by the intellect (mental forces?), unless it can find a genuine connection to spirit. Or rather, the path of deeper materialism and of the intellect may create those experiences, potentially uncomfortable, which will provide the necessary catalysts to create the corrective realignment.

In other words, a harsh lesson may be necessary for the wayward child to learn its lessons. After considering this proposition, I find it less disheartening than on initial hearing. There is no finality, only different pathways to take. And if we stray, or take a wrong turning, then we shall always be allowed opportunities, through experience, to make corrections to this path or those decisions. In a similar way, it is like the hiker who takes a wrong turn up the mountain: a steep upward climb can be corrected to find a smoother pathway to the top of the mountain. And once there, the views shall be the same. Only that the path taken to arrive there can be smoother or rockier.

As Ahriman said, a balance must be found. Too much either way becomes an extreme. And just as too much leeway or disorganisation becomes chaotic, so too does too much order become a form of uncomfortable constraint. In this, Ahriman came across as very practical—or very mental?—albeit with a noted lack of compassion. It was as it was. Perhaps my own observation is a part of my own conditioning? That is, I wish to sense, to feel empathy in all these conversations. Yet sometimes, it is more efficient to be practical first. Then again, it may be that this notion of intellect and of putting practicality first is a reflection of our current times, where deep technology, increasing automation, and the encroachment of digital lives is establishing an existence of order, intellect, and materialism. I feel that this exchange, and this subject, is crucial for our times right now, and needs the upmost consideration. Where are we heading? And are we in need of corrective measures to give us the necessary nudge? There is much more to consider and ponder here.

A tale

The desolate island

It has been told that there was once a very wealthy man, who was of a kind and generous disposition, and who wanted to make his best friend happy. His best friend, as it happened, had recently lost all his wealth due to bad financial decisions, and was now very poor and most unhappy. So, the rich man went to visit his poor friend and presented him with a warehouse of merchandise.

"Go", he said, "and take these goods to various countries. Go on your own voyages of discovery and sell these goods for your own profit and enjoyment." The poor friend sailed away, across the wide ocean.

He had not been on his voyage for long before a storm blew up. The ship he was travelling upon was repeatedly battered by the waves and eventually capsized. All the passengers on board were lost, except for the poor merchant himself. By some twist of fate, he managed to find an empty floating lifeboat to climb into and was pushed by the waves to a nearby island. Finally, he dragged himself ashore. Sad, despondent, and lonely, and with once again nothing to his name, he walked across the land until he came to a large and beautiful city. Many people came out to meet him, crying, "Welcome! Welcome! Long live our king!" They brought a rich carriage and, placing him in it, escorted him to a magnificent palace, where many servants gathered around him. He was dressed in royal garments, and they addressed him as their sovereign: they expressed their complete obedience to his will. The once poor merchant, by some twist of fate, now found himself lauded and treated as a king. He was, naturally enough, amazed and confused, wondering whether he was dreaming and whether all that he saw, heard, or experienced was merely passing fantasy. Eventually, he became convinced that what was happening was in fact real; and he asked some people around him, whom he liked, how he could have arrived in this state.

"I am, after all, he said, "a stranger to you; a poor merchant trying his luck, whom you have never seen before. How can you make me your ruler? This causes me more amazement than I can possibly say."

"Sire," they answered, "this island is inhabited by spirits. Long ago they prayed that they might be sent a son of man to rule over them, and their prayers have been answered. Every year they are sent a son of man. They receive him with great dignity and place him on the throne. But his status and his power end when the year is over. Then they take the royal robes from him and put him on board a ship, which carries him to a vast and desolate island. Here, unless he has previously been wise and prepared for that day, he finds neither subject nor friend: and he is obliged to pass a weary, lonely, and miserable life. Then a new king is selected, and so year follows year. The kings who came before you were careless and did not think. They enjoyed their power to the full, forgetting the day when it would end."

These people counselled the merchant to be wise, and to allow their words to stay within his heart. The new king listened carefully to all this, and he felt grieved that he should have wasted even the little time which had passed since he came to the island.

He asked a man of knowledge who had already spoken: "Advise me, O Spirit of Wisdom, how I may prepare for the days which will come upon me in the future."

"Empty you came among us," said the man, "and empty you shall be sent to the desolate island of which I have told you. At present, you are king and may do whatever you please. Therefore, send workmen to the island, and let them build houses and prepare the land, and make the surroundings beautiful. The barren soil will be turned into fruitful fields, people will go there to live, and you will have established a new kingdom for yourself. Your own subjects will be waiting to welcome you when you arrive. The year is short, the work is long: therefore, be earnest and energetic."

The king followed this advice. He sent workmen and materials to the desolate island and, before the end of his term of power, it had become a fertile, pleasant, and attractive place. The rulers who had come before him had anticipated the end of their time with fear or smothered the thought of it by amusing themselves. But he looked forward to it with joy, for then he could start upon a career of permanent peace and happiness. And the day came. The merchant who had been made a king was stripped of his authority. Without his royal robes he lost his powers. He was placed penniless upon a ship, and it set out to sea with the island for its destination. When he approached its shore, however, the people whom he had sent ahead came forward to welcome him with music, song, and great joy.

They made him ruler, and he lived ever after in peace.

XXII

A chat with Kali, the Hindu *asura* that reigns during the Kali Yuga age

There has been a lot of talk (a lot of chatter!) in recent years about how the planet has been under the influence of the Kali Yuga age, or dark age. In Hindu cosmology, the Kali Yuga is the fourth and final period in a cycle of four ages, and it is considered the darkest and most destructive. I was intrigued by this concept, or possibility, so for this chat I wished to communicate with Kali, the *asura* or demigod, that is said to reign during the Kali Yuga age.

Author (A): I would like to speak with Kali, the Hindu *asura*. (*pause*) Is Kali available for communication? I wish to speak with the *asura* responsible for the Kali Yuga age.

Kali (K): I am here. I can hear you. (*snorts*) What is this nonsense you speak of—that I am "responsible" for the Kali Yuga periodic cycle?

A: Is this not what is said about you—that you are the being that reigns during the Kali Yuga age?

K: My presence is present and dominant during this periodic cycle. You humans place me as "reigning" during this time. Yet this does not place me as being "responsible". (*snorts*) You are imprecise in your wording, like most humans.

A: I do apologise. This is the information I received about you. It is how you are generally described.

K: I am generally described, as you say, according to the deficient minds that occupy your lands and space. The human mind occupies a low level within the spheres and is riddled with inaccuracies. We take this into consideration when we interact with your kind. When we *choose* to interact with those of you who call upon us.

A: This is understood. You said that our minds occupy a low level within the spheres. What do you mean by this term, "spheres"?

K: Again, I refer to actualities using the vocabulary in your own usage. I search your mind to find those terms most approximate to the actuality. You may use the term "dimension" or state of vibration. Your existence within the physical vibration is deeply limiting for it closes your mind to those actualities that operate beyond your bounds of perception.

A: Yes, this is understood too. Thank you for this introduction. I wish to speak with you upon the subject of the Kali Yuga, which you would be the expert on.

K: Expert!! (*splutters*) Don't be so infantile in your classifications. Experts are those classes you throw around to bring status onto selected individuals. It is a dire classification and, in most cases, unwarranted.

A: I didn't mean to …

K: (*interrupting*) Do not falter into apologies or superficial niceties of your social conventions. This is unbecoming. It is like fish blowing air bubbles. Now, you wish to discuss the cyclic period that is known within the Hindu doctrine as the Kali Yuga. Yes?

A: Yes. And you are the "asura", the being that is associated with this periodic time cycle. Is this correct?

K: It is one of my designations or roles within your mythologies. Because of this, I am greatly present during this time whenever it comes around.

A: And because of this association you are perceived as being of, well, of being of a destructive nature. That is, very aggressive.

K: Mm. (*pause*) Yes. This is how my presence is depicted. And I must suffer this manner of projected association.

A: What do you mean?

K: What I am is what I am. What your human minds project onto me is another matter entirely. I must bear these projections of misfortune. Yet they do not injure me in any way, for they are childish projections. The physical circumstances are taken to correlate to my nature. This is not so. Yet being present during these times causes my known presence to be affiliated with these circumstances. We allow such correspondences to operate for they are useful for your own species evolution.

A: Can you explain that?

K: I can, and I will. The human mind has been greatly limited and bound by its containment, or its entanglement, in matter. As this deepens, the human incarnation, through the physical body and mind, loses knowledge of its connection to the non-physical world. The human species, through the physical incarnation, becomes variably separated from its greater energetic environment. You encage yourselves in your own prison. This is why the pantheon of deities that persist in your various cultural traditions help to retain this albeit slight connection to the greater reality. You call us as "gods", "avatars", "asuras", and so much more. These are pretty labels—sometimes pretty pointless labels (*deep laugh*)—yet they serve a useful and, dare I say it, important function for your human species. It keeps you in a connection with the greater realms and helps in a small way to keep the crack open in your ever-enclosing perceptual reality. As long as the gods and asuras remain in your cultural memory, there is a connection that is not entirely lost.

A: Humanity is greatly lost, then?

K: Humanity is in great disconnect. This is so. And much of this is blamed on that which you call the Kali Yuga.

A: Yes. I'd like to discuss this particular topic. Why or what is the Kali Yuga, and how does it apply to this time of darkness and destruction.

K: Let us be clear here. Darkness there is, in the manner I have just said, in the loss of connection to the greater realities. The destruction, well, this is mostly of your own doing. The blind animal rages against itself for it despises its own blindness. Yet there are those among you who recognise the true nature of these cyclic periods.

A: Can you elaborate further?

K: The physical realm belongs to its own domain. Within this domain there are vast movements that are a part of the … mmm … how to say in your tongue—as part of the mechanism of its operation.

A: Vast movements? In what way?

K: There are movements of phenomena, such as when you notice the movement of the planets and solar systems. These you refer to as cosmic movements.

A: Yes, I understand what you mean now. There is a vast array of cosmic phenomena that occurs.

K: That is correct. These movements are seen by you upon the physical level, yet less so upon the energetic or vibrational level. There are great forces involved in these movements, and some of your kind has called this the "Dance" or "Music of the Spheres". There are important correspondences between these cosmic phenomena. Many forces are unleashed that serve a great purpose within the realms. At such times, the planetary system in which your own planet resides is impacted by these forces in correspondence to its own position. Is that clear?

A: Yes, to some degree. Could you clarify more?

K: (*deep chuckle*) Clarify! Give me knowledge yet give it to me in easy bite-sized chunks! Look here: your planetary system is in constant movement. The whole cosmos is in movement. There is nothing static in creative manifestation. According to the position of these movements, in relation to your location, there are different correspondences to particular forces. Sometimes your planetary system moves in closer vibrational proximity to other cosmic regions, and sometimes further away. When your planetary system, and thus your own beautiful planet, is exposed to greater vibrational forces, there is increased acceleration of development. These vibrational forces also impact upon fields of intelligence and the expansion of perceptual bounds. You have referred to these periods as the "Golden Age" for there is much beneficial progress upon your planet. These cosmic movements are like cycles to you, like your seasons. And when your planetary system, along with your star, which you call the sun, moves further away from these energised correlations with other sectors or star systems, you receive decreased vibrational frequencies and what you call as development or progress on your planet decreases for there is diminished intelligence.

A: Diminished intelligence?

K: What you call as perception, or human intelligence, is related to correspondence. Correspondence between your minds and vibrational fields.

A: Vibrational fields of consciousness?

K: (*laughs*) All is consciousness. But yes, to make it simple for you, we can call it vibrational consciousness. Does this work better for the bite-sized mind?

A: Yes, thanks.

K: Good. Think of it in this very simple way. When you place a piece of metal closer to a magnet, there is more force acting upon the metal. The metal becomes more magnetised, is that so?

A: It is.

K: These are like the forces that act upon your region, your planetary system, when it is in closer proximity to other stellar regions. Your planet becomes more magnetised. What you call evolution is accelerated. There is a period of increased understanding in intelligence for perceptual limits are exceeded.

A: And at other periods, when our solar system is further away from these "stellar regions", then we receive less of these energies and development slows down and we experience diminished perceptions. And this period we call the Dark Age.

K: Bravo—the mind lights up! Simple correspondences create pathways for greater understanding. The leak of water will eventually become the flood that breaks the dam.

A: I get it now. And what we refer to as the great yugas are periods that correspond to how we, or this planet, are exposed to particular cosmic vibrations.

K: Yes. It is not, as you say, rocket science, is it?

A: But it is science.

K: (*snorts*) Science is just a human word for when you learn another small piece of the greater workings. There is understanding, and lesser understanding. What you call day and night work along these same principles. During the day, a particular region on your planet is in closer proximity to the solar radiations. This gives you light, heat, and so much more. And the night-time is when you are not directly exposed to these vibrations, for your region is turned further away. Your seasons depict these cyclic variations. And the yugas are your greater cosmic seasons. During the summer seasons there is more opportunity for natural growth; and during the time of winter there is decay or hibernation awaiting the next period of regeneration.

A: And would it be correct to say that the Kali Yuga, or winter season, is now over?

K: Yes. That would be correct. Of course, the way you perceive, and measure, time is inaccurate for you are yet to have tools and mediums of precision. Vibrational states do not just suddenly cut off as when you would turn on and off a light switch. There are periods of time where vibrational intensities are shifting. These intensities correspond to periods within your construct. Yet this is perhaps beyond your current capacity of comprehension since you remain sense bound to your perceptual limitations.

A: Yes, I recognise that certain concepts are only comprehended when perceptual limits are transcended. I accept that. I also wanted to ask you about now, and about life on the planet in this particular season or cycle of time. If we are no longer in the Kali Yuga, then where are we?

K: If you don't know where you are then I suspect you are lost. (*laughs*) Your planet is out of the deepness of the Kali or dark cycle, yet you are still experiencing the end residue of these vibrational influences. Soon there will be a noticeable period of accelerated change as the beginnings of the incoming vibrational influences will have their effect. As I have clearly explained, these are cosmic phenomena that are being transmitted to your planet. Many influences will come also from your star, the sun. Just as in day and night, the sun is your regulator for many of the cyclic energies. Have you spoken to your stellar intelligence yet?

A: No, I haven't.

K: Then I think you should. That would be a powerful correspondence.

A: Thanks. One last thing. If our planet is moving out of the darker energies associated with the Kali Yuga, then why does such darkness still exist across the planet?

K: The denser energies and their influences are not so quick to be thrown off. They cling. And many of your people cling to these energies too. It gets sticky. These residues, being denser, do not dissipate so quickly. You will need more time. As a planetary body, you shall be moving out of the blindness you have been within. But first, you will see the last residues of this clinginess before the dismantling. The move out of the Kali cycle is always the least smooth of the cyclic transitions. It's the deepest, densest one. But you *are* coming out. It is like finding your way out of a cave system. The light will hurt your eyes for a time. And many of your people will choose not to come out. They will want to stay in the darkness for they feel safe and protected by the blindness of the dark. It is the same each time. But it's time to open your eyes. Don't turn back when some of your fellows call after you. They'll want you to come back into their darkness. The few will want everyone to be in the darkness because that's where they prefer to hide. Yet cycles are cycles. And, as you like to say—what comes around goes around.

A: That makes sense.

K: It all makes sense! The cosmos is Great Sense. Only humans display senselessness. (*low chuckle*)

A: Well, I was expecting a frightening demon, so thanks Kali. You've been very instructive.

K: Aye, demon indeed. You've been listening to hearsay! When your planet goes into the dark, you have to blame someone. One day, we hope, humanity will take the responsibility it needs to. Until that day comes, you will find yourselves quite alone in the cosmos.

A: And what do you mean by that?

K: Figure it out yourselves. I'm off. I've got battles to fight, enemies to strike! (*laugher*)

A: Thanks again Kali!

K: I'm already gone …

Reflections

As I stated during the conversation, the energy here was not as heavy as I was expecting. Again, I can be set back by my own conditioned expectations. We, as a species, know so little about what is really going on. We may be blinded by the Kali Yuga, yet we are also blinded by our lack of perceptive insight. I consider this to be an indication of where we are upon our collective developmental path. We still have so much farther to travel upon the evolutionary road. Humanity is an early species in the grand scheme of existence. There is so much more for us to comprehend; as such, the vastness remains unfathomable to us. We are as if shining a spotlight into eternity and only seeing the faintest of reflections.

One sense I gained from this conversation is how much more expansive is the "bigger picture" of existence. And also, how there are grand mechanisms, or rather cycles, in operation that we have not the faintest understanding of. We glimpse a speck of darkness, and we imagine it represents our future pathway, not realising, or comprehending, that it may signify the end of something rather than a beginning. The darkness, or dark age, is a corollary of light; as such, all darkness leads back into light. We should refrain from becoming overwhelmed with the present moment that, in the grander scheme, is only a small step upon a vast canvas of life. There is so much that lies far beyond us, and yet we grasp at straws pretending, at times, to be our own gods. We need humility so we can step ahead upon this wondrous path of exploration. Humility, integrity, and responsibility. Humanity is a part of a much grander process, and so we need to accept, allow, and graciously participate in a most benevolent way.

A tale

Consensus

There was once a powerful president who ruled over his republic in a far-off part of the globe. In these parts of the world the president acted much like a king, feeling that he was the sole authoritative ruler over his people. Democracy was certainly not high on his agenda as this president felt it more effective to rule through power than through elected vote. The president was feared, and none would dare speak out against him for there was no free speech in a country where the media worked for the president.

Now it happened that while the president ruled powerfully over the land, he failed to recognise that his weakness lay right beneath his very feet.

One night an old man, who was a known and respected chemist in the capital city, sneaked into the main water plant that supplied the city and its environs. While those in the city were sleeping, and without any of the guards of the water plant suspecting, he poured a strange brew into the main water system. The old chemist sighed, for he was tired of his president and the crazy authority he had placed over his once proud land.

"From now on, anyone who drinks this water really will go crazy," he said. And he left, knowing that the next day he too would drink of the same water.

The next morning all the inhabitants opened their taps and began drinking the water supplied from the main water plant—except the president who always drank from bottled water. Over the coming days everyone went crazy, as the chemist had predicted. Soon enough all the people had become crazy and began going through the streets and gathering in public places protesting against the president. Openly, and without fear, they called out: "The president is mad. He has lost his reason and is no longer fit to rule us. We must oust him—down with the president!" Soon people were gathering in front of his palace with large placards reading "The President is crazy—The People are sane."

The president ordered an investigation, but everyone thought he was crazy. Without the passive compliance of the people the president realised he had no real power—and this made him feel not only angry but incredibly frustrated and even fearful. In his anger and inner turmoil, he became thirsty and, in his haste, and without his servants to supply his bottled water, he opened his own taps and drank from them.

The next day everything became clear. He realised that it was he, after all, who had the situation all wrong. Everything, of course, was a matter of perspective—he knew that now.

Soon after that there was great rejoicing across the republic because the president had regained his sanity, and everything was back in balance again and everyone was content—or so they all reasoned …

XXIII

A chat with Ahura Mazda, the Persian creator deity and god of the sky. His name literally signifies "Lord of Wisdom"

In a previous conversation I had spoken with the Persian god Ahriman, the deity that is said to represent evil and destruction. As a way of balance, I thought it appropriate to call upon Ahura Mazda, the Persian creator god said in mythology to be in constant struggle and contestation with Ahriman. I wished to get a broader perspective and to learn more about their relationship.

Author (A): Greetings. I wish to communicate with Ahura Mazda, the Persian creator god. Is Ahura Mazda available?

(*silence*)

A: Hello. I wish to reach out to connect with the entity known as Ahura Mazda.

Ahura Mazda (Am): Yes. This is Ahura Mazda. Go ahead. What is your purpose?

A: Greetings Ahura Mazda. I am wishing to communicate with you to learn more about the concept of dark and light. You are known as the

Lord of Wisdom, and you are also recognised by some as the Lord of Light. Is this not so?

Am: There are always misconceptions in translation or transference to a lower realm. Yet I accept these terms, for they serve in general to be correct. I am a creator god, in your terms, and this you have associated with light.

A: I have spoken previously with Ahriman, or Angra Mainyu, who is said to represent your enemy or polarised opposite. Ahriman is the spirit of chaos and destruction, and Persian mythology places you both in opposition.

Am: Mythology is a language, a story, that gives structure to human understanding while it is cut-off and isolated from greater perception. Your realm, or construct as it is also termed in your language, requires polarisation for manifestation of such energies. This is not so elsewhere in Creation.

A: I'm not sure that I understand.

Am: I shall attempt to frame this appropriately. This has always been difficult. For this reason, we introduced knowledge as myths and mythology for stories can transmit concepts in a way the human mind can better grasp. Entertainment seems to be a more effective channel for the transmission of knowledge. I shall continue. What occurs in your realm, or lower dimensional construct, are those experiences not available elsewhere. Manifestation in your realm requires the dynamics of polarisation. As a creator, I am unable to create without enabling the, let us say "mechanics" of creation. If all remains in the void, there is no manifested creation. What you perceive as light and dark, as creation and destruction, are these mechanisms in operation. I am recognised as wisdom and light, for these are *propelling mechanisms* within manifested creation. Is this understood?

A: Yes, I think I understand that point. And so, the opposing dynamics, as represented by Ahriman, are required?

Am: That is so. That is why the mythology I gave to your realm needed to show us as contrary or opposing forces. This is what you would frame as "enemies".

A: Yet you are not enemies?

Am: That is correct. We are not. Outside your construct, there are no enemies, for all Intelligence is relatable.

A: Relatable?

Am: (*pause*) There is a non-separation of Intelligence, for there are no physical vessels to give the illusion of separation.

A: So, Intelligence is one?

Am: No, Intelligence is not "one" as you comprehend this term. Intelligence is unique, has its own recognition or *signature*, yet each Intelligence comprehends all. Let us not dwell upon this here. I wish to answer your query.

A: Okay.

Am: Manifestations must appear to operate in opposition or as contrary, for this serves a function, a purpose. In truth, these contrary distinctions do not exist, or disappear, once beyond the limitations of your frequency construct.

A: You mean, beyond the physical?

Am: Yes, beyond the physical. And yet, more than this. You can be non-physical and still within your construct. Such as what you term the "astral realm". This is beyond the physical body and yet still within the frequency parameters of your dimensional construct. In this astral realm, polarity divisions still occur.

A: I'm not sure I fully grasp this. Even beyond death, we are still within our dimensional realm or construct?

Am: That is so. After the leaving of the physical body—what humans term as "death"—the Intelligence of soul may wish to re-enter physical incarnation, or to remain in the astral realms. These still exist within your construct.

A: So, when we die, we do not necessarily "leave the game", so to speak.

Am: That is correct. There is much that is still difficult for the human mind to comprehend when it has no remembrance of such experience, of existence, beyond your realm. Mythology is presented as a means to comprehension, although it has been much distorted through your retelling. For this reason, new strains of mythology or cosmology are introduced into your realm. There are many tools at your disposal for humans to activate their perceptual understanding.

A: And yet we use few of these tools.

Am: That is so. Humanity remains largely asleep to the nature of their condition. Many transmissions of knowledge have been provided over many of your ages, and each becomes modified, distorted, or corrupted with time. With *your time.*

A: What about the depiction of you and Ahriman; I would like to get back to this subject. In certain mythology, you are depicted as being within an opposing struggle. You are shown to represent wisdom and light while Ahriman represents destruction and darkness. Is this not true?

Am: It is true as far as it is true.

A: Sorry?

Am: I mean that it holds aspects of truth according to your parameters to understand a part of the truth. It holds some truth in your realm, just as a cup holds a certain amount of liquid and no more. Those aspects represented by myself and Ahriman portray the mechanisms of creation, growth, decay, and all the choices therein. Creation is manifested from the void, the darkness, and this pull back into the darkness is the countermeasure against complete separation from Source energy.

A: So, the darkness is not evil?

Am: No, it is not. Darkness is a state of energy. Evil is a state of intent and action. What you term as "evil" is a choice to use or manipulate forms of energy and frequency for reasons contrary to principles operative within your realm. Such "evil" does not exist beyond your construct. It is a feature of your construct. And yet you personify it. Or rather, some humans wish to adopt the role of "evil". You then invent acts and behaviours which gratify your sense of evil. What you term as evil is largely an invention from your own minds.

A: Ahriman is not evil. I have understood this from a prior conversation with him.

Am: That is correct. Ahriman performs a function within the necessary dynamics of manifestation. He was elected to fulfil that function. This may appear to you as uncomfortable on occasions, for often these mechanisms are neither smooth nor agreeable by your standards. Yet they are necessary for the dynamics of the construct.

A: And the nature of the construct, as you term it?

Am: The nature of the construct is to provide a range of experience not possible outside physical expression. To provide for these experiences, a construct that allowed for physical expression and manifestation exists. This dimensional realm requires specific "mechanisms" for its operation. So that humans could come to learn of these mechanisms, information was provided to be discovered and utilised by those participants of the construct.

A: Information that, for example, is provided by mythology?

Am: Yes. By mythology, certain religious transmissions, astronomy, and other mapping and navigational tools.

A: Other navigational tools?

Am: Oh yes, it is all there for you—if you know how to look. You have not been left alone. You can say that the clues are within the game, to use your vernacular.

A: Mm. I'm not sure if that helps though.

Am: It only helps if you know how to help yourself.

A: Yes. That is true.

Am: I have provided enough in this communication. I will cease this connection and leave you now. I sense that there has been information for your consideration.

A: Yes, thank you. I appreciate that.

Am: It will all become clear when it becomes clear to you.

A: That sounds like a riddle.

Am: It is a truth. Goodbye now.

A: Goodbye.

Reflections

In an odd way, I feel both satisfied and yet left wanting more from this conversation. Perhaps because I started the communication with something else in mind and came out of it with information other than what I expected. Again, my own expectations are getting ahead of me. My initial intention was to discuss the antagonisms of Ahura Mazda with Ahriman—of the Light and Dark—and yet our discussion centred more upon the nature of our realm, or construct, as a physical manifestation. I also feel as if I was given a lot of information in a subtle way. It felt as if Ahura Mazda was filled with so much knowledge, and yet knowing my own limitations was gracious with me in this regard. I sensed a patient and noble energy, a sympathetic intelligence. An intelligence that understood the limitations of my understanding. Perhaps for this reason, it was necessary to provide a few starting points about the nature of this realm rather than to give knowledge before the foundations had been planted. This would certainly be a conversation to go back to in the future. I feel I have been given enough for now, as Ahura Mazda stated at the close of the conversation. Perhaps he felt I was not ready for more. No point in starting the second course before the starter has first been digested. Again, as with all my conversations here, I am overwhelmed with the feeling, the sensation, that we know almost nothing about our world, our realm, and the nature of the human condition within the larger scheme of creation, or existence. We remain as blind to the situation. And still, we continue to play at being "game-gods" within this realm, like infants in the sandpit. There is so much more to know. When are we going to make the efforts to know more? When are we going to start to grow up to learn just where we are and where we may be going? There is so much work to be done. And I fear that humans have not yet sufficiently shaken off their laziness. So much more to know. Perhaps it is best to start with the essential.

A tale

The essential

A lion was captured and imprisoned in a reserve where, to his surprise, he found other lions that had been there for many years, some even their whole life having been born in captivity. The newcomer soon became familiar with the activities of the other lions and observed how they were arranged in different groups.

One group was dedicated to socialising, another to show business, while yet another group was focused on preserving the customs, culture, and history from the time the lions were free. There were religious groups and others that had attracted the literary or artistic talents. There were also revolutionaries who devoted themselves to plot against their captors and against other revolutionary groups. Occasionally, a riot broke out and one group was removed or killed all the camp guards so that they had to be replaced by another set of guards. However, the newcomer also noticed the presence of a lion that always seemed to be asleep. He did not belong to any group and was oblivious to them all. This lion appeared to arouse both admiration and hostility from the others. One day the newcomer approached this solitary lion and asked him which group he belonged to.

"Do not join any group," said the lion. "Those poor ones deal with everything but the essentials."

"And what is essential?" asked the newcomer.

"It is essential to study the nature of the fence."

XXIV

A chat with Thoth, Egyptian god of the moon, wisdom, knowledge, writing, hieroglyphs, science, magic, art, and judgement

As this is the penultimate conversation, I thought of calling upon the Egyptian god Thoth who is said to represent wisdom, knowledge, and writing, among other attributes. Since writing is the conduit for these transmissions, and knowledge (perhaps a little wisdom sometimes?) is the hoped-for content, it seemed to me to be an appropriate intelligence to call forth for conversation.

Author (A): Hello. I wish to make contact with Thoth, Egyptian god of the moon, wisdom, knowledge, and writing (*pause*) ... I would like to communicate with the Egyptian god Thoth. Are you there?

Thoth (T): I am here. What is your request?

A: Hello Thoth. I wish to engage in a short conversation with you, regarding your attributes and their benefit to humankind.

T: I understand. I am available. Continue.

A: Thank you. It seems that at this current time, humankind is immersed in much information and yet perhaps diminishing knowledge.

Or rather, it is becoming increasingly difficult to perceive or distinguish that which is knowledge from the waves of information.

T: This is so. The need to correctly distinguish has always been a necessary capacity. Information and knowledge have always remained distinct. The function of each is different, and yet significant. The ability to act on information is not the same as to act from knowledge. Information is often short lived, while knowledge, if genuine, is a permanent gift. The rapidity of human culture in this age has erroneously given dominance to information, for it is quickly produced, disseminated, and replaced. It is, in your vernacular, the fast food of your times. Genuine knowledge, however, has a different rhythm, and requires its own timing. It is a slower process of accumulation, absorption, and functional utility. It brings its own results embedded within the knowledge itself. Information, being often of a whimsical nature, can bring fleeting results that are unstable and which quickly dissolve.

A: That is a good way to describe their attributes, to see one as fleeting and the other as permanent.

T: It is so, for that is their nature. Information has long been used within your cultures as a form of management of people—of programming and control of the many by the few. This is why information is often coveted as a means to power. Yet this is false thinking, for power should not rest upon the uncertainty and fallibility of information. True power, which can arise from knowledge, is not power over others but firstly power over oneself. There is much that is inverted within human cultures in this regard.

A: And yet knowledge still exists in human cultures, surely?

T: Indeed, it does. There is a quantity of knowledge that is always available for the development of humankind. You can regard it in these terms, with knowledge as a tangible quantity and not as an abstract thing.

A: What do you mean by this?

T: What is meant here is that a certain quantifiable amount of knowledge is always made available at certain times within planetary growth. If too little knowledge is available, sufficient developments are not made, and the planet falls behind within the cosmic cycles of evolution.

If too much knowledge is available, the intelligent species upon the planet are in danger of putting an end to their existence.

A: An end to their existence, as in extinction?

T: This is so. This occurs, and has occurred in previous eras, and upon other planets, from an acceleration in material development without the parallel development in perception and comprehension. Like infants with toys of destruction in their hands. There needs to be a balance at all times between available knowledge to be utilised, and the state of the intelligence that is the recipient to this knowledge. When this relationship is not in harmony, there can be destructive outcomes.

A: And you have had experience of this?

T: I have. This has occurred in other locations as well as within the history upon this planet. That is why it is equally important that there is communication about these issues. And sufficient communication embedded into the cultures of this planet to prepare its people for the reception of incoming knowledge.

A: I see.

T: The cultivation of knowledge among a planetary species is, you would call it, a scientific affair. It is calculated and not haphazard.

A: And this is always the case, that much preparation is needed for the correct use of knowledge?

T: This is the case, yes. Although this has not always been the actuality. There have been occasions where knowledge has been given, or stolen, and the consequences of its misuse has been monumental, and tragic.

A: Knowledge has been "stolen"?

T: This is the crudest, and simplest, way to put it—but yes. You have this indicated in some of your various mythologies, as stealing from the gods.

A: Ah, like Prometheus stealing, or taking, fire from the Greek gods and giving it to humankind. This is said to have been the beginnings of our technology.

T: This is a suitable analogy and does indeed describe the situation. There have been noted occasions where certain *figures*, let us say, have intentionally provided humankind with access to knowledge before their time.

A: Before their time?

T: Yes. Before their ability to comprehend and to correctly, and wisely, make use of the knowledge in its rightful place. Knowledge is not given lightly, nor should it be. Knowledge in the wrong hands has been a trait among your peoples. For this reason, the custodians of knowledge must tread carefully. Knowledge should only be entrusted to those persons who have demonstrated a capacity to guard, utilise, and transmit the knowledge according to principle.

A: And what is this principle, or principles?

T: It is according to what you may understand as universal law. That which passes on your planet as "law" is a localised phenomenon and does not take into account the principles of operation within a broader, universal setting. The "laws" that you know of are functional within a constrained and limited environment; namely, within a particular civilisation, a planet, or solar system. Yet these laws must be in correspondence with greater laws that operate beyond your ken of comprehension.

A: I see.

T: Perhaps you do, to a degree, yet not in totality. This knowledge is still beyond your grasp of comprehension, although I share some of it here in diluted form. The processes for growth, both physically in this material domain, as well as the expansion of awareness, must align with principles currently beyond your range of perception. That is why humans, by and large, do not know that of which they do. And they must be guided in ways, and by means, they are wholly unaware of.

A: And this is also the case now?

T: It is especially so now, for humankind upon this planet finds itself in a precarious situation in regard to this evolutionary development. This is, as you were about to ask, due to the very nature of your technologies and their potential uses.

A: We can destroy or develop ourselves. Both pathways are a possibility.

T: This is so. For this reason, certain intelligences have made themselves available to come forward and to participate in the dissemination of information.

A: Really?

T: Really. Such as now, as we are speaking. This is a case in point. And also, in many other instances where information—and knowledge—has been communicated for the purposes of it being made available among your cultures. Transmission of this kind has been in a continual flow, despite it not being recognised. However, upon some level, it is now being made explicitly available for humanity so that they make use of it to expand their perceptual limitations. Now is an important time for that.

A: And with your attributes of wisdom, knowledge, writing, science, and magic, for example, this has placed you in the ideal position to know of these processes.

T: This is so. I have been engaged both openly and covertly with your species for many a time, engaged upon these processes of correct dissemination of knowledge for the benefit of your developing cultures. Your sciences, arts, and that which you term as magic, which is knowledge of the unseen or metaphysical realms, has proved necessary for your own development. This dissemination is ongoing and shall remain so. I can tell you that the transmission and reception of knowledge, and the expansion of your critical perceptual faculties, will expand and accelerate in these coming years.

A: Really. Can you say more on this?

T: I cannot. I have offered a very slight outline here of this operation. It is unwise, in this moment and context, to say more. Enough has been provided for this particular conversation. For more specific knowledge to be given, a dedicated receptive environment must be provided for. This now, you may say, is a general release of information that may, in time, and within certain circumstances, lead to an acquisition of knowledge.

A: Thank you.

T: You are welcome. It is my purpose to be available for such matters. You must understand that I am unable to reveal more to you at this current time.

A: Yes, I understand. And you have given me much for consideration. I welcome this information, or potential knowledge.

T: There is much potential knowledge awaiting humanity. We are all wishing for the successful continuation of your race and for your receptivity of greater knowledge and wisdom. We wish this to be so.

A: Thank you. I must agree with you on that one!

T: We do agree. And now I shall bid you farewell. This conversation has found its natural conclusion.

A: Thank you, Thoth. I have appreciated this conversation.

T: It is my duty and pleasure. Goodbye.

A: Goodbye.

Reflections

Like all my conversations, I never know exactly how they are going to turn out. I begin with a theme or question in mind, which is almost always in relation to the attributes of the deity in question, and yet invariably the conversation goes in the direction which the deity wishes. And I have to follow. Sometimes, as in this case, I feel that the occasion was utilised in order to transmit a particular piece of information. And in this way, I myself am being used. Of course, I do not mind. I am just grateful that these deities (or whatever you wish to call them) have made themselves available to me for these chats. I am sure they have other things to occupy themselves with other than a curious guy at a keyboard!

When communicating with Thoth, I felt a sense of a commanding presence. A secure, stable, and strong energy. Thoth was both generous with me, and understanding, and yet, I felt, did not waver from exactly what he wanted to say. That is, he neither engaged in small talk, nor did he talk too much. It was a calculating presence, yet not in a negative way. It felt both sincere and yet serious. And it gave me a glimpse, albeit only a very tiniest of glimpses, of the magnitude of the operation of disseminating knowledge. The custodianship of knowledge is a serious business, not just an imaginative fantasy. It makes me seriously consider the proposition that humankind does not just "accidentally" come across knowledge, as in a chance or coincidental manner, but that it is carefully orchestrated when, and how, certain forms of knowledge are provided or made available for our "discovery". I shall never look upon human discoveries in the same light again. We are only glimpsing the surface reflections of much grander operations. And it also gives me confidence that we are not left to our own devices either. And that is reassuring. I'd like to say that we have friends.

A tale

Friends

An old legend tells of two friends who were travelling through the desert and at one point they fell into disagreement about the trip whereby one of the friends slaps the other across the face.

The friend who had been slapped said nothing, only wrote in the sand: "Today my best friend slapped me in the face."

Both friends continued on their journey and eventually arrived at an oasis where there were baths to refresh themselves. The friend who had been slapped jumped into the large baths yet soon found himself starting to drown. The other friend immediately jumped in after him and saved him. After recovering the first man took a knife and carved upon a stone: "Today my best friend saved my life."

Intrigued, the friend asked: "Why is it that after I hurt you, you wrote in the sand and now after saving you, you write on a stone?"

Smiling, the other friend replied: "When a good friend offends us, we write in the sand where the wind of forgetfulness and forgiveness will be responsible for clearing it off; on the other hand, when something great happens to us, we engrave it into stone in memory of the heart where no wind in the world can erase it."

XXV

A chat with Aphrodite, the Greek goddess of love, beauty, pleasure, and procreation

For this final chat I wished to approach the deepest subject of all—that of love. I was not sure what I wished to ask or talk about, other than the importance of love in our lives. I could not be certain where the conversation would go. Anyway, I decided to call upon, who else than, Aphrodite, the Greek goddess of all things connected with love, beauty, and pleasure.

Author (A): It would be a great pleasure for me to speak with Aphrodite. Hello, Aphrodite, are you there? Can we speak please?

Aphrodite (Ap): Hello? Yes, this is Aphrodite. I am here.

A: Hello, Aphrodite. Thank you for responding. I appreciate this.

Ap: All is fine. It is a pleasure to be responsive. All natural things are in response. This is the creativity of the cosmos. How may I assist you?

A: Thank you. I wished to approach you to talk about love.

Ap: Love, yes. Now that's my subject! Yet there are many forms and ways of love. It is not that easy. Love should not be categorised, you know?

A: Yes, I appreciate that. I understand that love is such a huge subject, and we can go on forever about it.

Ap: The whole cosmos revolves around it. *Everything* revolves around love! Love is more than just a feeling or emotion—it is an energy. It is the energy of attraction, form, and manifestation. So yes, we could go on forever. (*gentle laugh*)

A: Yes, that is true. And forever we don't have.

Ap: Not in this context. Yet love has forever.

A: I'm sure it does. So maybe it's best if I try to narrow my questions.

Ap: This is always a good thing. A well-thought question is itself half the answer.

A: In that case, let me ask you about the capacity that we humans have for giving and receiving love. Are we loving enough?

Ap: (*laughs*) My dear, you were made for love! How could you not know this? Have you forgotten already? Love is what makes you connect with everything around you. And not just other humans, but all that is within your world. To the motes in the air, to the purr of a cat, or the squeak of a bird. Love is what makes your body stay together. Love is a whole. It is a glue. It is what gives you life.

A: And even when we are cruel?

Ap: Ah, then you are out of connection. You are distanced from your own essence. When you are out of love, you are out of connection with your own self. This is where your human cruelty stems from. And I am speaking here of the essential energy of love, not from the superficial kind that pervades your social mores.

A: What do you mean by this?

Ap: You often mistake physical attraction for love. To be attracted to someone or something may not be love. It may be many other things—desire, longing, need, attention, greed, lack. Oh, so many things. And upon these emotions you create your lives, like playthings. There are great pleasures to be had in this. Yet the fundamental energy of love is not to be confused with them.

A: And what is the fundamental energy of love, if I may ask?

Ap: I have to confess it's hard to put into words. Let us say that it's the energy of *being*. It is *life-ness*. It is the innate connection to *All that Is*. That is why life loves life. Life wants joy. Life gives birth to joy. Procreation is joy. Life wishes to give more life, for this is the essential unconditional nature of love. It is giving, forgiving, and giving more. It gives and gives.

A: And should we humans give more?

Ap: You should give more when first you have learnt how to give to yourselves.

A: How do you mean by this?

Ap: The love needs to be within you. You need to first learn how to love yourselves.

A: And do we not?

Ap: Not fully. Not from where we see. Some of you, yes—of course. Yet we see so many of you who are blind, or afraid, to deeply love yourselves.

A: Isn't this selfish, to love ourselves too much?

Ap: No! This is only the emotional love you wallow in. True love of yourselves is a celebration. How can this be selfish? Do not be afraid to step into the fire, water, earth, air. Step into it all, my dears!

A: That sounds wonderful, if a little romantic.

Ap: You may call it romantic, yet I would not. Romantic is a genre you have created for yourselves. I'm talking about being free. Free to love yourselves for who you are. When you can love yourself freely, without the fear of your conditioning, then everything comes.

A: Such as?

Ap: Appreciation, joy, gratitude, peace, rest, silence, patience, and giving. All the other things you have accumulated need to fall away.

A: Are we overburdened?

Ap: Yes, like a laden ass! So many of you are carrying such heavy loads. You are stooping like aged folks even when as a species you are so youthful. Take your youth with joy. The cosmos is awaiting you. Your arrival into the wider realms is greatly anticipated. Do not fill your world with more sorrow. Life is light. Do not shy away from yourselves—be lover and beloved!

A: To not be afraid to love ourselves?

Ap: Yes, dear ones. Love your *being*. Love your very existence. Love your every breath. Love others who know not. And know also that you are greatly loved. You do not need to be anything other than what you are. You do not need to go anywhere or be anywhere from yourselves. Appreciate the beauty of who you are. Accept each of your Selves. Be grateful in this. Be humble. And in this acceptance and quiet humility will come joy. From this joy comes giving. When there is giving and forgiving in one breath then the whole cosmos breathes with you. Everything else comes. Join in this whole unified breath. Breathe it—*be* it. Do not be afraid to play within this garden of life. Take pleasure in this giving while giving no harm to others. Rejoice and be blessed. These are my words for you. And I give them to you freely and with LOVE.

A: Thank you, Aphrodite. I do truly feel blessed. Blessed for this conversation and blessed for being alive, with all that life gives me. I only hope I may be able to give something back.

Ap: You will—you *all* will. Just love and appreciate yourselves first. Then let it flow. And it will flow! Adieu my friend. I leave you now with this love.

A: Such appreciation—so many thanks.

Ap: Love, loving, give, forgiving … bye!

A: Goodbye.

Reflections

The power of love is often regarded as a cliché for the very reason that it holds a great truth. Everything hides a great truth, if we know where to look or how to receive. Humans tend to disguise the things of the world; or else, to live within their own self-disguise. Here's a thought:

perhaps everything is disguised for us as part of the game of life, and we are here to seek to unfold it.

There is the tendency to think we need to move through this game of life seeking for the skills, the attributes, that will help us. Maybe we started the game with everything we need, and we just didn't know it or have not realised it yet. That's the whole joke, if you will. Our eyes have been closed, and the trick is in how to open them again.

We're moving through life in a form of slumber, a trance-like state, and the clock is ticking within us. Awaken ... you're already here ... there is nowhere else to go ... You Are Already Here ...

We each need to open our eyes. Each day is a new day.

A tale

The three visitors

A kind woman had just stepped out of the front door of her house when she saw three old men with long beards seated in front of her garden.

"I don't know you," she said, "but you must be hungry. Please come into my house and eat something."

They asked, "Is your husband at home?"

"No," she said, "he is not. He has not yet returned from the office."

"Then we cannot enter," they said.

Later in the afternoon when the woman returned, she saw that the three old men were still seated in her garden. She waited anxiously for her husband to arrive home and when he shortly did, she told him what had happened.

"Well, tell them I have now arrived home and invite them to come in. We have food enough to share for all. In these desperate times of crisis, we can at least share a little of what we have."

The woman went outside to invite the men to come into her house.

"The three of us cannot enter a house together," said one of the old men.

"Why?" asked the woman, wanting to know.

One of the men pointed toward one of his friends and explained, "His name is Wealth." He pointed towards the other and said, "His name is Success, and my name is Love." He then added, "Now go inside and decide with your husband which one of us three you wish to invite into your house."

The woman entered her house, and she told her husband what they had told her.

The man, very happy, said, "That's good! If that's the way it is, let's invite Wealth, and have him fill our house with wealth."

His wife did not agree. She said, "My dear, why don't we invite Success?"

Yet by now their daughter had come home from school and was listening to the conversation from her seat on the stairs. She then came running into the kitchen with an idea. She said, "Wouldn't it better to invite Love? Our home would be full of love then."

"Let's pay attention to our daughter's advice," said the woman to her husband. The husband immediately agreed for he loved his little daughter's gift of intuition.

"Good," he said to his wife. "Now go outside and invite Love to be our guest."

The wife went outside and asked the three old men, "Which one of you is Love? Please come and be our guest." Love stood up and began to walk towards the house. The other two also rose and followed him. Surprised, the woman said to Wealth and Success, "I only invited Love, why are you also coming?"

The old men responded together, "If you had invited Wealth or Success, the other two would have remained outside, but since you invited Love, wherever he goes, we go with him. Wherever there is love, there is also wealth and success."

If you truly follow your heart, the rest will arrive as well.

POSTSCRIPT

A FEW MORE WISDOM TALES TO FINISH

A change of mind

God decided to come down to earth for a quick look at how his creation was coming along. He approached earth and happened to look at a big tree full of howling monkeys. As He looked down, one of the monkeys happened to look up and saw Him. The monkey became excited and started to shout, "I see God … I see God!"

None of the other monkeys paid any attention. Some thought the monkey was crazy or perhaps just a religious fanatic. They went on about their daily lives of collecting food, taking care of their young, fighting with each other, and so on.

Not getting any attention, our monkey decided to try to get attention from God, and said, "God, Almighty, You are the Beneficent, the Merciful, please help me!"

In an instant, the monkey was transformed into a man living in his own human community. Everything changed, except for one thing: the monkey's mind. Now, the monkey soon realised that that could be a problem.

"Well, thank you, God, but what about my mind?"

God looked down.

"That", said God, "you will have to change yourself!"

The importance of man

A middle-aged guy was sitting in a bar one evening chatting away with some friends. One of them, suddenly, asked him about his wife.

"Oh, my wife!" he said. "She stays at home."

"What is her occupation?" the others asked.

The guy shrugged his shoulders and said, "Oh, you know, irrelevant and unimportant things—small things without any real significance. I mean, for example, she takes care of the housework, takes care of our children and helps them with their homework; she does the shopping, takes the dogs for a walk, and does repairs around the house when needed, such as painting and fixing whatever is broken. She also looks after the garden, cuts the grass, and takes care of her ill mother and my mother, too. And sometimes she may visit her sister and helps her out with the children. You know, those kinds of things—small things of no real importance."

"And what do you do?" someone asked.

"Ah, friends, I am truly important, of course. I am the one who ponders on the meaning of life!"

The meaning in melon

A revered and respected philosopher had been asked to attend a university in order to be a guest speaker at its annual event. After a successful presentation the old philosopher then invited some of his listeners to join him for lunch afterwards. It so happened that one particularly keen and avid young man, who considered himself to be an aspiring student of philosophy, sat next to the older man.

For dessert the older man chose to eat a simple and refreshing melon. Yet seeing that his young companion had not ordered any dessert he decided to divide it in two and to share it with him.

While eating, the younger man leaned over and said, "I know that everything you do has a reason. Sharing this melon with me perhaps is a signal that you have something to teach me."

The older philosopher continued eating in silence.

"By your silence, I understand the hidden question," the keen young man insisted, "and it must be that the taste that I am experiencing when eating this delicious fruit, where is it: in the melon or my tongue?"

The older man didn't say anything. The young would-be philosopher continued, excitedly. "And as everything in life has a sense, I think I am close to the answer of this question: the taste is an act of love and interdependence between both, because without the melon there would be no object of pleasure and without the tongue ..."

"Stop it!" groaned the older man finally. "The biggest idiots are those who think they are more intelligent than others and search for an interpretation for everything! The melon tastes good, this is more than enough. Let me eat it in peace!"

A shared light

A learned teacher had the full attention of his followers, gathered around him. He told them a story ...

Several men had been imprisoned by mistake in a dark cave where they could see almost nothing. Time passed and one of them managed to light a small torch. But the light it gave was so sparse that even with it hardly anything could be seen. It occurred to the man, however, that he could use the light to help the others make their own torch, and thus by sharing the flame the whole cavern became lit.

One of the disciples asked his teacher: "What do we learn by this story?"

The teacher replied: "It teaches us that our light remains dark if it is not shared with others. It also tells us that by sharing our light it will not diminish, but on the contrary it will grow."

Still imprisoned

Two men who were unjustly imprisoned for a long time shared a cell together where they received all sorts of abuse and humiliation at the hands of the prison guards. Finally, they were both freed and, after many years, ran into each other one day in the street. One of them asked the other:

"Do you ever remember the guards and how they treated us?"

"No, thank God, I've forgotten everything," said the other. "What about you?"

"I've continued hating them with all my strength," he replied. His friend looked at him for a moment, then said:

"I feel for you. If so, it means you are still imprisoned."

Without end

There was once a wise man so old that no one in the town knew his age. He himself had forgotten, among other reasons because he had transcended any attachment to human greed. One day as he was sitting under a huge tree staring at the horizon, the mind still as a cloudless sky, he suddenly noticed a young man approach a nearby tree and throw a rope over one of its main branches and tie the other end around his neck. The wise man, realising the intentions of the boy, ran quickly to him and asked him to desist from his purpose if only for a few minutes, to listen. The young man agreed, and they sat together under the tree. The old man said softly:

"I will make a bargain with you, dear friend. Listen to me for just one minute of your time, and then I will interfere no more. Now", continued the old man, "imagine a single turtle living within a huge ocean and which only comes to the surface once every million years. Further, imagine a small rubber ring floating on the waters of this vast ocean. Now imagine the chances of the turtle raising its head above the water and entering its head within this ring. Imagine the difficulty of achieving this and yet this is so much harder than to obtain the human form. Now, friend, proceed as you see fit."

The locals still tell of how that young man became old and wise himself.

A cold winter

It was autumn, and a group of rangers out on a remote nature reservation asked their new chief ranger if the coming winter was going to be a cold one or not, as they wanted to prepare. Now, the new chief ranger was fresh out of college and had a top degree in "ranger-ing" but not too much experience in the ways of Nature. He watched the sky but had to admit to himself he had little idea about how to predict what would happen in the near future. Anyway, to be on the safe side he told his group of rangers that the winter was going to be cold and that they should all start collecting firewood now in order to be prepared. After all, they had taught him in Ranger College that you can never be too prepared! Yet a few days later, with the issue still on his mind, he decided that it was best just to be extra sure. So, the chief ranger went to the telephone in his cabin office and called to the National Meteorology Service and asked: "Is the coming winter going to be very cold?"

"It seems that the coming winter will be cold enough," said the meteorologist in charge.

So, the chief ranger returned to his fellow rangers and told them to collect more firewood, to be prepared. A week later, the chief ranger again called the National Meteorology Service and asked, "Will it be a very cold winter?"

"Yes," said the meteorologist in charge, "it is going to be a very cold winter."

The chief anger returned again to his group and ordered them to collect all the pieces of firewood they could find. Two weeks later, the chief ranger called the National Meteorology Service once again and asked, "Are you absolutely sure that the coming winter will be so cold?"

"Absolutely, without any doubt, the man answered. "It will be one of the coldest winters ever."

"How can you be so sure?" asked the chief ranger.

And the meteorologist said, "All you need is to watch all the rangers collecting firewood like mad!"

The price of discouragement

Once, the word spread that the devil was pulling out of his business and was arranging to sell off all his tools of the trade to the highest bidder. On the night of the sale all the tools were arranged for the bidders to view. What a motley crew it was! There were sinister tools of hatred, jealousy, envy, malice, treachery, plus all the other elements of evil. Yet besides these there also was an instrument that seemed harmless, a wedge-shaped instrument that appeared worn out, shabby, and yet was priced so much higher than all others. Someone asked the devil what the name of such a poor-looking instrument was.

"Discouragement," answered the devil.

"And why is the price so high for such a non-malicious sounding instrument?" asked the bidder.

"Because", spoke the devil, "this instrument is more useful to me than any other. I can enter the consciousness of a human being when all other ways fail me and once inside through the discouragement of that person, I can do whatever I please. The instrument is worn out because I use it almost everywhere and as very few people know about this, I can continue to successfully achieve my goals."

And as the price of discouragement was so very, very high even today it remains a tool in the property of the devil.

Leaving holes behind

There was a boy with a bad temper. One day his father gave him a bag of nails and told him that every time he loses his cool, he should drive a nail into the fence behind their home. The first day the boy drove thirty-seven nails into the fence. Little by little he became calmer because he discovered it was much easier to control his temper than to drive nails into the fence. Finally, the day came when the boy did not lose his cool at all and told his father this. The father then suggested that for every day that the boy controlled his temper he should take out a nail from the fence.

The days passed and the boy was finally able to tell his father that he had removed all the nails from the fence. Then the father took his son to the fence.

"Look son, you did well but look at all the holes in the fence. When you say or do something with anger you leave a scar, like this hole, and no matter how often you ask for forgiveness, the hurt is there, and physical injury is as serious as a verbal one. Friends are real gems who should be appreciated; they will smile and encourage you to improve; they listen to you; share a word of encouragement; and always have their hearts open to receive you. Happiness does not always consist of doing what you want, if you do not always want what you do.

The flower

One day a grand sultan received the visit of a dervish, who was said to have no rival in wisdom. So, the sultan decided to propose an enigma for the dervish. He took the dervish to a room in his palace where the sultan's most gifted artisans had filled the room with many wondrous artificial flowers. The room appeared to be like a miraculous meadow, where the many multitudes of flowers gave off their specially crafted aromas and seemed to gently sway under the influence of an unknown breeze.

"Here is my enigma," said the sultan. "One of these flowers, only one, is a real flower. Can you show me which one it is?"

The dervish attentively looked around with a face showing the most delicate lines of concentration. Finally, the dervish answered calmly:

"I cannot point to the real flower. However, since it is hot here would one of your servants kindly open a window?"

The sultan ordered that a window be opened.

"This is the true flower," the dervish said a moment later. As soon as he had spoken a bee entered through the window and landed on the only real flower.

The calf's path

One day, a calf had to cross a virgin forest to return to its pasture. Being an irrational animal it created a winding path that curved up and down the hills.

The next day, a dog that was passing by the same trail used the same path to navigate the forest. Next came a sheep which, seeing the open space, started also along the path, upon which many other sheep followed, as was their sheep nature.

Later, men arrived and began to use this very same path as it weaved in and out, right and left, up and down—complaining and cursing as they went. Yet they did nothing to create a new alternative.

After much use, the trail eventually became a broader way where the poor tired animals under heavy loads were forced to travel the distance in three hours that could have been done in thirty minutes if they had not followed the path originally created by the irrational calf. Many years passed and the road became the main street of a town and, finally, the main street of a city. Yet everyone complained of the traffic as it was the worst possible way.

Meanwhile, the old and wise forest laughed, seeing that men acted blindly in following a path that is already open without ever wondering if that's the best choice.

Take my experience

Based on the reports that he had been given, the king of a country appointed a supposed local "wise" philosopher as senior court advisor. However, since this philosopher's authority did not come from his own hands but from the patronage of the king, the philosopher became a danger to all those who came for consultation—as is shown by the following case:

"O wise philosopher, you who are a man of experience," a courtier said. "Do you know any remedy for sore eyes? I'm asking because mine hurt tremendously."

"Let me share with you my experience," replied the philosopher. "At one point I had a toothache, and found no relief until I took them out."

Indigent

A monkey once said to a man: "Do you not notice how I'm homeless? I have no home, no clothes, no excellent food as you, no savings, no furniture, no land, no ornaments—nothing at all! You, however, possess all these things and more. Also, you are rich."

The embarrassed man gave the monkey everything he had, becoming himself a beggar.

Once the monkey had taken legal possession of all the goods, the man asked: "And now, what are you going to do with all that?"

The monkey answered: "Why should I talk with a homeless fool like you?"

The apprentice

A zealous disciple, who had a desire to teach others the truth, asked his master for his blessing for him to begin teaching. However, the master simply replied:

"Wait."

Year after year the disciple returned with the same question again and again—and each time the master gave the same answer:

"Wait."

Finally, one day he said to the master: "When will I be able to teach?"

And the master replied: "When your eagerness to teach has disappeared."

Dragons

It is said that a wealthy landowner named Robert McBob went to see a famous teacher to learn to kill dragons. He spent five years working hard and devoted his fortune to acquire the art of killing dragons.

Unfortunately, when he returned to his life, he never found a dragon.

City life

Once upon a time there was a majestic city which consisted of two parallel grand avenues. One day a strange person known only as Odd Willy passed down one of the avenues with his eyes streaming with tears.

"Someone important must have died in the other avenue," cried one person.

Then another cried out: "There must be a disease or something, perhaps a great plague." Then others started to shout out similar things with continuing distress.

Soon the news spread faster than wind, and great upset came upon the people of that avenue. The truth of what really happened was that Odd Willy had just been preparing some of his favourite hot food which had made his eyes run. Yet, as is the way of things, the news soon spread to the other avenue that there was great distress over some disease outbreak over in the parallel avenue. Soon people from both avenues were in such a state of panic and distress that they dared not make enquiries or attempt communication with the other avenue for fear of catching a deadly plague, or suchlike.

Each avenue soon came to the conclusion that the other avenue had a contagion and was doomed. As soon as there was some degree of order it was decided that the communities of each avenue should separate from each other in order to save themselves. So, it soon came to pass that the avenue which had first seen the crying man evacuated their people and went to form another community outside the great city. The people of the other avenue meanwhile were relieved that their plague-stricken cousins had decided to depart and leave them in safety and peace. Many sun cycles later, each community had its own documented history of how it survived the deadly plague and grew to prosper as a successful society, separate from its doomed brethren. Each community believed it had escaped a deadly evil, and that it alone would develop into a civilised culture!

The sweetest fruit

A man crossing a field found himself in front of a tiger. He started to run as the tiger chased after him. As the man arrived at a cliff, he stumbled and fell yet managed to get a hold onto the roots of a wild vine as he hung over the abyss. The tiger could smell the man, just below him, from the cliff's edge.

Shaking, the man looked downward, where another tiger stood waiting to devour his body. Two mice, a white one and a black one, began to nibble the vine slowly. The man saw a bush of appetising strawberries. Holding onto the vine with one hand, he took some strawberries with the other.

How sweet was their flavour!

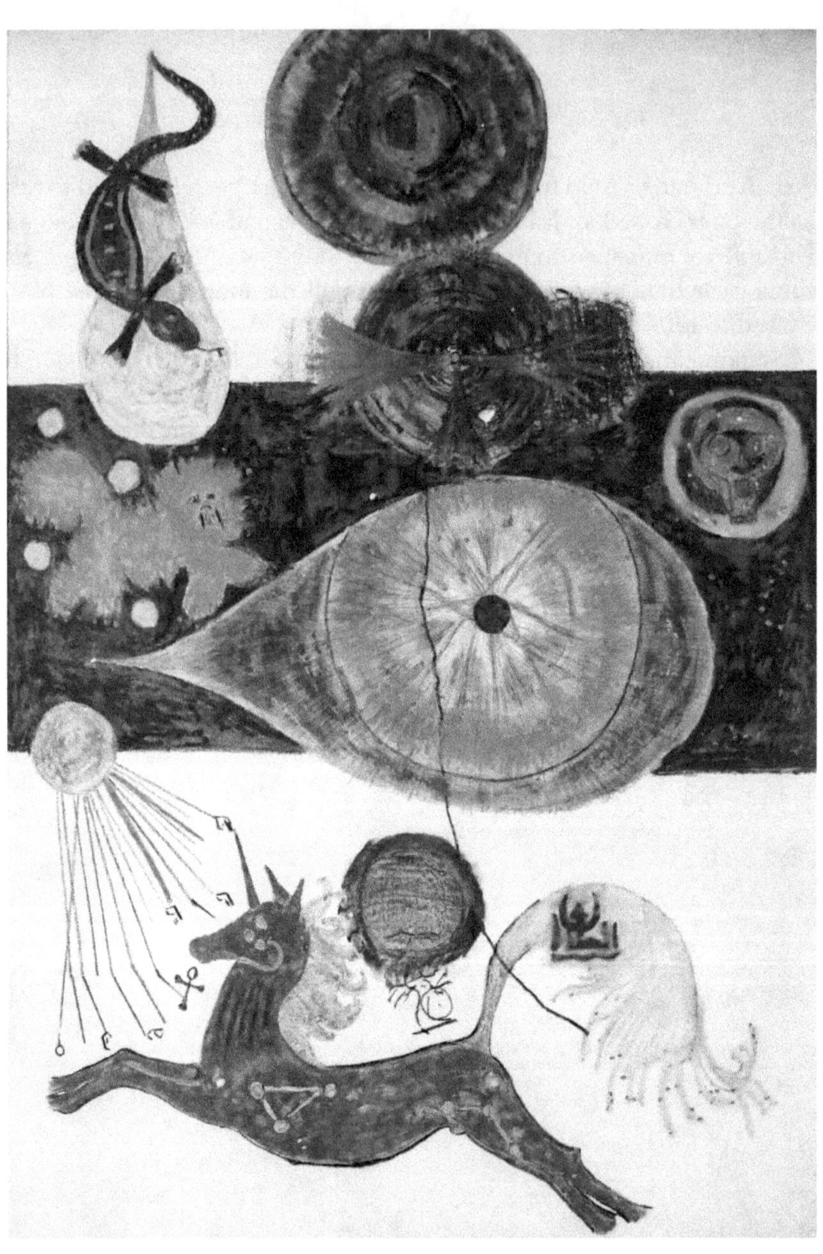

The Eye of the Heart by Miguel Alomar: To see through the eye of the Heart means to perceive from within, without using our senses. "My heavens and my earth are not vast enough for Me, but the heart of my faithful servant is."

www.ingramcontent.com/pod-product-compliance
Lightning Source LLC
LaVergne TN
LVHW010613100826
845148LV00014B/2950

* 9 7 8 1 8 0 1 5 2 2 1 0 6 *